Golf Digest's
ULTIMATE DRILL BOOK

Also by Jim McLean

Golf Digest's *Book of Drills*
The Complete Idiot's Guide to Improving Your Short Game
Golf School
The Eight-Step Swing
The X-Factor Swing

Golf Digest's®

ULTIMATE DRILL BOOK

OVER 120 DRILLS That Are Guaranteed to Improve

Every Aspect of Your Game and Lower Your Handicap

Jim McLean

GOTHAM
BOOKS

GOTHAM BOOKS

Published by Penguin Group (USA) Inc.
375 Hudson Street, New York, New York 10014, U.S.A.
Penguin Books Ltd, Registered Offices: 80 Strand, London WC2R 0RL, England
Penguin Books Australia Ltd, 250 Camberwell Road, Camberwell, Victoria 3124, Australia
Penguin Books Canada Ltd, 10 Alcorn Avenue, Toronto, Ontario, Canada M4V 3B2
Penguin Books (NZ) Ltd, Cnr Rosedale and Airborne Roads, Albany, Auckland 1310, New Zealand

Published by Gotham Books, a division of Penguin Group (USA) Inc.

First printing, October 2003
10 9 8 7 6 5 4 3 2 1

LIBRARY OF CONGRESS CATALOGING-IN-PUBLICATION DATA
McLean, Jim, 1950–
    Golf digest's ultimate drill book : Over 120 drills that are guaranteed to improve every
    aspect of your game and lower your handicap / by Jim McLean.
        p.   cm.
    ISBN 1-59240-018-3 (hardcover : alk. paper)
    1. Golf.   I. Golf digest.   II. Title.
    GV965.M1755   2003
    796.352—dc21   2003006482

Printed in the United States of America
Set in Garth Graphic with Rotis Sans Bold
Designed by Sabrina Bowers

I dedicate this book to *Golf Digest* magazine, the best golf publication of all, with the most experienced staff. Thank you for believing in my first drills book and carrying through with this new publication.

CONTENTS

FOREWORD

By Len Mattiace

My first year on tour was in 1993, and I played lousy. I knew I needed help and had to find a golf instructor fast. My good friend, Brad Faxon, suggested that I see Jim McLean at the Doral Golf Resort and Spa in Miami, Florida.

Right from the start I hit it off with Jim. Not only is he a great instructor, but Jim is also a super coach. (He has learned from the greats like Byron Nelson, Claude Harmon, Ken Venturi, Sam Snead, Johnny Revolta, and Jack Burke, Jr. and coaches from other sports like John Wooden and Bobby Knight.) He knows the proper positions of the swing and can communicate ways to get there. And this is why this book, Golf Digest's *Ultimate Drill Book,* is so valuable.

Doing the drills is essential to each player improving their game and shooting lower scores. For example, going into the 1995 Tour Qualifying School, "the 6-round pressure cooker," Jim and I had a certain plan to execute the L Drill after each round, with 40 balls. I did it and the results were 16 under par, finishing 18th place and qualifying easily for the tour! Since then, I've improved every year and with Jim's help finished 18th on last year's tour money list, earning $2.2 million. I have won two PGA Tour events and finished runner-up in the 2003 Masters, losing in a playoff after a final-round 65.

Whether I am down working with Jim at Doral, at home practicing, or on tour competing, you will see me do these drills and you should do them too! Do the drills that are relative to your needs and see your scores get lower and lower.

Good luck on the links always.

Jacksonville, Florida

INTRODUCTION

When I wrote the original Golf Digest's *Book of Drills*, there was no organized manual or book containing proven drills. I had seen many great teachers use wonderful drills to help students, but none of them had put them all together into one complete reference resource. So, during the winter of 1984, I wrote that first book in Orlando, Florida, in my spare time when not playing in tournaments. I'll never forget that experience. My wife Justine allowed me to use the living room of our apartment, where I had the full manuscript laid out on the floor. And it took that entire off-season for me to organize things.

Later that winter, I shot accompanying photographs. There was a chapter for each part of the game; the idea was that readers could find several good drills for whatever problem they had and solve their swing and shot-making problems through intelligent, honest practice. The beauty of that book was that everybody could find something productive in it, no matter what they thought about swing technique.

Back then, drills were not nearly as popular as they are now. I found that out when I pounded the streets of New York City looking for a publisher. No one bought the idea.

It was not until the 1987 Orlando Golf Show that I found someone who liked my book—Jack McDermott of *Golf Digest* magazine. But it was not until 1990 that the book finally came out. That was because so much additional work had to be done, including reshooting the photographs and then having an artist do drawings based on them.

Thankfully, the brutal work paid off. The original Golf Digest's *Book of Drills* was an immediate success and, to this day, is still in hardback and has been reprinted fourteen times. The response was tremendous: Not only did average golfers offer accolades, so did top tour pros and teachers.

In the years following the publication of that book, I learned or invented many more drills, and in 2001 I came to another crossroads in my career. After wondering why no new drills book had been written, I decided to ask *Golf Digest* to step up to the plate once again.

What you now hold in your hands is a guidebook to golf improvement, since drills or practice exercises serve as a catalyst to learning, allow you to correct faults that sneak into every player's swing from time to time, and learn new tee-to-green scoring shots.

All of my instructors, at each and every school site, use drills to teach what I consider are the eight vital steps in a good golf swing, inclusive of what I call the Corridors of Success and the critical X-Factor positions. Let me explain, so that you are very clear about these instructional points.

The eight most logical steps of the swing, as determined by the study of top golf professionals and amateurs, are as follows:

Step One: The first move in the backswing.

Step Two: Halfway back.

Step Three: The three-quarter position of the backswing.

Step Four: The top of the backswing.

Step Five: The move down to the ball.

Step Six: Impact.

Step Seven: The early follow-through.

Step Eight: The finish and rebound.

I believe that learning to groove these ideal positions through drills is the true shortcut to good golf. However, there are not eight exact positions you must achieve. The ideal swing patterns must require allowances for your own personal differences, since there are always differences in great golf swings. To represent this, I came up with the Corridors of Success—parameters within which I like to see any swing fall. For example, on the backswing, I might prefer that the left wrist be flat, although small variations are okay. A flat left wrist at the top is nice, but it is not a fundamental. Whatever area of the swing needs work, you can improve and groove it by working on drills, all designed to help you learn a new action or correct a faulty one in your technique.

I have a detailed system for teaching the game, and I do stress the importance of the X-Factor to many students working to improve through drills. The X-Factor is a proven concept that first takes into account the differential between the turn of the hips and the turn of the shoulders—your torque. It's how you turn, not how much, and what counts most is the gap or differential between the two turning actions. The *X-Factor* book discussed power positions from setup to finish and focused entirely on body motions. *The Eight-Step Swing* focused on how to teach and diagnose everything in the golf swing. Both books required a tremendous amount of research, which I have loved doing.

I'm happy that many of my philosophies and top drills come to the surface in Golf Digest's *Ultimate Drill Book*. This comprehensive instructional text contains what I call "Timeless Winners"—evergreen drills I have been teaching for years—plus well over one hundred new drills. What's more, this book contains photographs throughout rather than illustrations, since all the "players" involved in this project agreed that it will better allow you, the reader-golfer, to use the instructional messages put forth in the text that follows.

Whatever your handicap, this book can help you reach your full golf potential. I make this profound statement simply because I have witnessed students improve greatly by doing drill work. By practicing these drills, you can zero in directly on problem points in your game or golf swing, and address these right away.

I take great satisfaction in knowing that this book's publication will also allow teachers to learn new ways to help their students get better at golf. Take it from me, drills have broad use and can be used by *all* golf instructors, regardless of their own individual swing theory. Furthermore, any drill in this book can be modified to produce slightly different feels and swing actions.

Drills even work for tour players. Just recently, Vijay Singh told me that drills from my first book helped him improve his golf swing. Vijay's comment was very rewarding, considering he is a former Masters and PGA champion. And throughout Tiger Woods's life, all of his teachers, from his father Earl Woods, to Rudy Duran, to John Anselmo, to Butch Harmon, have had him use practice drills.

One of the drills I helped invent, the Stop-And-Go Drill, was a significant help to Tiger as he made swing improvements in the late 1990s with Butch Harmon on his way to becoming the world's leading golfer. Let's hope this drill, along with many others in this book, will help you bring your game to peak-performance level. All you have to do to accomplish this goal is to determine what area of your swing or shot-making game needs improvement, go to the relevant chapter containing specific cure-all drills, then sacrifice some playing time for practice time.

Good luck in your self-improvement journey.

Jim McLean
Miami, Florida

Golf Digest's

ULTIMATE DRILL BOOK

Chapter 1

TIMELESS WINNERS

- *Favorite drills for every golfer, from my original bestseller, Golf Digest's Book of Drills, designed to help you develop technically sound setup, swing, and shot-making fundamentals*

All of the practice drills you are about to learn are extra-special because they have stood the test of time. These drills are still being used by golf instructors at the Jim McLean golf schools, many top teachers around the country, and of course, myself.

These "timeless winners" serve as a good introduction to the myriad other drills contained in this very comprehensive book—each designed to help you improve your setup, swing, or shot-making game. Regardless of your handicap (or, in case you're a teacher, your swing theory), you'll find all of these drills— from the Grip-Pressure Drill, to the Stop-And-Go Drill, to the Hands-Leading Chipping Drill, to the Wedge-Stroke Putting Drill—extremely practical and easy to practice.

You'll have to practice regularly to achieve major change. But your time will be well spent. I know from the experience of thousands of golfers that using drills in practice sessions will help you master the proper golf moves and hit better shots. These are the golf motions and positions that will accelerate your learning curve.

GRIP-PRESSURE DRILL

Problem: The golfer either grips the club too tightly or holds the club too lightly.

Result: The golfer tenses up vital golf muscles and drains power from the swing, or sacrifices high speed for low control.

Goal: To determine what degree of "personalized" grip pressure allows you to generate high clubhead speed and maintain full control of the golf club throughout the swing.

Practice Procedure: Start by gripping the club very lightly. Label your lightest grip pressure as "1," on a scale of 1 to 10. Next, grip progressively more firmly until you give the handle a big squeeze, reaching 10 on my scale. I invented the 1–10 scale in the 1980s to help golfers quantify the feel in their hands. As you proceed through my scale, give each degree of pressure a number.

Next, hit some shots, each time gripping more lightly than more firmly, until you find the grip pressure that allows you to hit the ball powerfully and accurately. That grip pressure number will probably be 4 or 5. However, there are allowable exceptions to the rule, according to my "Corridors of Success" leeway philosophy. The bottom line is: Find the grip pressure that gives you the best results, and nine times out of ten that will be lighter than what you've been using until now.

Constantly identify the feel of your personal grip pressure, so that you hold the handle the same way out on the course and give yourself the best possible chance to hit pro-standard shots. One more thing: Maintain constant grip pressure from the start to the end of your swing. This simple tip may become your best link to good play.

Tailoring the Tip: You can also vary pressure in each hand as you play intentional hooks and slices, which most golfers do not realize. Grip the club lightly in the right hand for a slice and lightly in the left hand for a hook.

Experiment with grip pressure until you find the hold that allows you to accelerate the club through impact into a balanced finish, like the one the player employs here.

INTERMEDIATE-TARGET DRILL

Problem: The golfer aims his feet, knees, hips, and shoulders left or right of the target, and often compounds the fault by aligning the clubface improperly.

Result: Either of these problems will play havoc with your shot-making ability, because to quote Jack Nicklaus: "If you set up incorrectly, you'll hit a poor golf shot even if you make the greatest swing in the world."

Goal: To learn to set up square to the ball, with the clubface perpendicular to the target and the bodyline parallel to the target line. Achieving this goal will enhance the probability of delivering the clubface squarely to the ball at impact and hitting on-target shots.

Practice Procedure: Like Nicklaus, pick an intermediate spot along the target line. I suggest anywhere from three feet to ten feet to thirty feet in front of the ball. Experiment in practice to see which "short target" makes it easier for you to set the club down correctly, then jockey your body into a matching square alignment position. Nicklaus actually looks at a spot very near the golf ball.

Once you determine your best intermediate target, lay a head cover down in that spot. Now, before hitting each practice shot, place that secondary target in your mind's eye and strike the golf ball directly over it.

When playing the course, pick out and focus on a divot, dark patch of grass, or bare spot that represents your intermediate target. Incorporating this "short target" procedure into your pre-swing routine, during practice and play, will help you establish correct club-body alignment positions that are likely to promote powerfully accurate shots.

TEE

When practicing, train yourself to line up to an intermediate target, such as a tee or a head cover in the path of your ideal shot.

TRIANGLE TAKEAWAY DRILL

Problem: The player exaggerates hand and wrist action early on in the backswing, causing the club to swing quickly away from center.

Result: These faults cause the arms to "disconnect" from the body, the swing plane to be wrong, and the tempo, timing, and rhythm of the action to be out of sync.

Goal: To find a way to learn and groove a one-piece takeaway that allows an imaginary triangle formed by your arms and a line across your shoulders to stay intact for the first part of the backswing. A technically sound takeaway action will encourage good positions throughout the swing, thereby increasing your chances of swinging rhythmically and delivering the clubface squarely into the ball at impact.

The Triangle Takeaway Drill in pictures: Look and learn.

Practice Procedure: Select your driver. Grip the clubshaft a few inches below the club's handle. Place the butt end of the club gently against your stomach, at a point just above your belt. Now practice making small swings, concentrating on keeping your arms close to your sides with the club touching your navel.

This drill, shown to me by instructor Jimmy Ballard, is used to help golfers maintain their triangle and learn to stay connected. It will help you groove a good one-piece takeaway action, employ a fuller turn, and create added power.

THUMBS-UP DRILL

Problem: After taking the club away correctly, the golfer dramatically over-rotates the hands and forearms, so that the thumbs of both hands point to the side, parallel to the ground.

Result: This is a mistake that will cause a dramatically negative domino effect, with the club ending up well behind the body on the backswing, giving the player virtually no chance of achieving square clubface-to-ball contact at impact.

Goal: To learn the correct position of your hands in the critical backswing and follow-through areas.

Practice Procedure: Swing back to chest level, making certain that your thumbs are angled up toward the sky. Hold that position for a few seconds, so you remember it and physically feel and groove it. Next, swing through to chest level, again making sure that your thumbs point at the sky. Hold that position.

Practicing this drill a few times a day will help you learn and master the correct hand-arm positions that are so vital to swinging the club along the proper path and plane.

Checking your thumbs on the back and forward swings is critical to training yourself to learn the proper hand positions involved in a good swing.

TWO-SHOULDER DRILL

Problem: The golfer fails to consistently set the club in an acceptable position at the top of the swing, with the shaft nearly parallel to the target line. The player's club may either point well left of the target at the top, in a laid-off position, or well right of the target, in a cross-the-line position, or it may finish well short of the classic parallel position.

Result: These incorrect at-the-top positions lead to faulty club-to-ball impact positions and redundant shots that usually fly far off target.

Goal: To learn how to consistently set the club in the parallel position (the clubshaft points down the target line), so that no manipulation with the hands and arms is necessary. You will find that the parallel at-the-top position gives you the best chance of achieving square contact with the ball and hitting shots at your designated target.

Step One

Step Two

Procedure: Without using a ball, make your normal backswing and stop at the top. Next, lower the club onto your right shoulder, so that your hands are about twelve inches from your right shoulder and the clubhead points at your target. You may choose to use the buddy system and have a friend confirm that you have matched these desired drill positions, or check yourself in a mirror. Next, swing through to the finish and hold that position. Lower the club onto your left shoulder and hold it there. The shaft should rest comfortably on the area between your neck and shoulder.

Keep practicing this drill until setting the club on your shoulder in the parallel position becomes second nature.

After you can easily swing the club into that resting position, stop the club at the top. Now simply raise the hands directly up, stopping when the hands are approximately five to ten inches above the shoulder. You are now in a powerful position at the top. The club is balanced, your arms and elbows are positioned properly, and you are relaxed. This all adds up to more speed and better clubface-to-ball contact at impact. Remember, it's okay to finish with the shaft on the shoulder, in a super-relaxed position that matches that of Tiger Woods and Ernie Els—two pros with super swings.

Step Three

Step Four

BASEBALL BATTER'S DRILL

Problem: The player fails to make a correct weight shift on the downswing, leaving too much weight on the right side instead of shifting into his or her left foot and leg.

Result: The player tends to hit a high slice. However, if he flips his hands over in a counterclockwise direction, he will probably hit a hook.

Goal: To learn the feel of a correct weight shift, so that the majority of one's weight is on the left foot at impact.

Follow this routine when practicing the Baseball Batter's Drill and you will learn to make a solid downswing weight-shift action.

Practice Procedure: Here's a great drill taught to me many years ago by legendary golf instructor Bob Toski.

Tee up a ball and assume your normal address position. Next, draw your left foot back to your right foot until your feet are virtually touching.

Start swinging, and just before you complete the backswing, stride forward with your left foot, like a baseball batter does when stepping into a pitched ball.

Practice this drill, actually hitting shots, until you feel and groove the correct downswing weight-shift action—in other words, one that produces good shots. You will be amazed at the results when you get the timing down correctly. Shot after shot will be near perfect. Remember to make that forward step while the club is still going back. Most golfers step too late.

STOP-AND-GO DRILL

Problem: The player wrongly triggers the downswing with a violent upper-body move or exaggerates the lower body slide.

Result: The player tends to come into impact with the clubface wide open and then slice the ball severely.

Goal: To synchronize the downswing action, so that the movements of the lower body, upper body, arms, and golf club are sequentially timed in a rhythmic manner. Moreover, to learn to let the hands go along for the ride, rather than letting them take control of the club.

Practicing the "stop" position (left) and the "go" position (right) will help you synchronize your swing.

Practice Procedure: Here's a simple but magnificent drill that I learned while watching multiple Senior PGA Tour winner Jim Albus practice.

Many years ago, I saw Jim stopping at the top, checking his position and then swinging. I tried it with students and gradually learned they could actually hit balls. When I first showed this drill to professionals, they were very skeptical, thinking a total stop was dramatically mechanical. Now I see many other teachers using the Stop-And-Go Drill that follows.

From your address position, swing the club back, stopping at the top of your backstroke. Be sure at this stage to check that your weight is balanced. Hold this position for a few seconds. Next, complete the swing and trigger a perfect chain reaction by rotating your hips and legs smoothly, but powerfully, toward the target.

As you practice this drill, you should start feeling the lower body change and the hands sync with the entire downswing action flowing on automatic pilot. I also like students to feel the hands drop down under the chin into and through the impact area.

This is an awesome drill for learning an efficient, on-plane move. It's also great for promoting good balance during the swing, so work hard practicing it.

TWENTY DRILL

Problem: The player loses power on the downswing because he fails to accelerate the arms. The player cannot improve swing speed.

Result: The player hits drives much shorter than he should.

Goal: To train the arms to swing the club powerfully, so that by the time the club swings into impact it is moving at high speed. Clubhead speed not only allows you to hit the ball longer, it adds height and carry to shots hit with the longer clubs.

Practice Procedure: Swing the club back and through twenty times in a row without stopping. Ideally you want to remain flat-footed through the impact zone. Some players are flexible enough to be able to swing all the way into the finish position while remaining flat-footed. I recommend you do this with a driver, swinging as fast as possible.

This drill trains you to feel how the body responds to the arms swinging and how the arms help swing the body.

Do twenty swings in the morning and twenty swings in the evening, for two weeks, and you'll see dramatic results.

Swinging back and through over and over will train you to employ a powerful arm-swing.

EXTENSION DRILL

Problem: Instead of letting the arms extend on the downswing, the player allows the right arm to cinch inward and the left arm breaks down into a faulty "chicken-wing" position.

Result: The swing arc is shortened and clubhead speed decreased, creating a loss of power.

Goal: To learn what I call the "extension position." In short, you want to extend the arms in the hitting area, so that a long flat spot is created, the swing arc widens, and clubhead speed increases.

Practice Procedure: Using a seven- or eight-iron, make small practice swings, each time concentrating very hard on stopping the club no more than four feet past impact. Next, look to see if both arms are extended, as former great player and teacher Johnny Revolta taught me to do, and make sure the clubface is square to the arc.

This is a superb drill for beginners and intermediate players, and a favorite at my golf schools around the country. After you can employ the perfect practice swing, begin hitting shots, being sure to stop at the "extension position."

Stopping when the club
swings a few feet past
impact will help you
incorporate extension
into your technique.

LOB DRILL

Problem: The player's swing lacks good tempo and timing, and he or she lacks an understanding of what makes their technique tick.

Result: The player plays "army golf," hitting a shot left of the target one time and right of the target the next.

Goal: To learn the basic vital elements of a good swing and how to make a more coordinated start-to-finish action.

This drill helps you quickly evolve into a better swing mechanic.

Practice Procedure: I learned this drill from former LPGA Hall of Fame member Betty Jamieson. It will help you become a better feel player and swing mechanic.

Practice hitting lob shots over a bush or tree located about five to ten yards in front of you. Make a full but very smooth, lazy swing, taking note of the role that each part of the body plays during the back and forward motions.

Betty would practice this one shot for hours. Regular workouts on the practice tee will allow you to increase your swing IQ and be a step ahead of your playing partners. Not only will you become a smarter, more rhythmic swinger of the club, you will be a great lob-shot player. You'll also be able to make solid, on-center contact with the ball off any lie.

HANDS-LEADING CHIPPING DRILL

Problem: The player fails to let the hands lead the club into the ball.

Result: He flicks his wrists in the impact zone, causing the leading edge of the clubface to hit the top of the ball.

Goal: To ingrain the correct hands-leading action into chipping your swing, so you hit solid, on-line chips that carry the fringe, "check," and then roll straight toward the hole.

Practice Procedure: This drill, taught to me by former Masters champion Claude Harmon, Sr., will make you a great chipper virtually instantly.

Take your normal chipping setup using your favorite club, and make sure your hands are slightly ahead of the ball.

Next, employ a short backswing. Before you start down, have a friend place the grip end of a club just in front of the ball. Hit the chip, letting your friend's club stop the head of your club just after impact. You will immediately sense a hit-and-resist feeling in both your hands and arms.

The moment your club is stopped by the grip end of your friend's club, freeze your position. Note that your hands are ahead of the ball. Memorize the sensation, so you'll remember to do the right thing on the course.

When Mr. Harmon taught at Winged Foot Golf Club in Mamaroneck, New York, he required every new golfer to work on this drill. His desire to see these small shots executed correctly in no small part led to hundreds of excellent golfers at his club. Jack Burke and his brother Jim, who both worked for Harmon, followed their former boss's instructions when moving on to Champions Golf Club in Houston, Texas.

When you arrive in
this position, stop and
feel the hit-and-resist
sensation so vital to
developing good
chipping skills.

BUNKER-PLAY TEE DRILL

Problem: The player digs the club too deeply into the sand.

Result: He fails to propel the ball over the bunker's lip and onto the green.

Goal: To take a shallower cut of sand, so that the shot floats over the lip and flies toward the hole.

Ken Venturi taught me this
Bunker-Play Tee Drill.

Practice Procedure: This drill, which I learned from former U.S. Open champion Ken Venturi, will help you solve your problem and get the ball up and in from the sand.

Push a tee into the sand, so that its tip is just above the surface. Place a ball on the tee.

Take your bunker-play setup, with the ball opposite your left heel.

Swing back.

Now swing down, trying to clip the tip off the tee. Almost immediately, you'll realize that to succeed you have to hit behind the ball with a shallow angle of approach. Knowing that will help promote the proper action. Now, just remember to take your new bunker-play technique to the course.

WATCH-THE-TEE PUTTING DRILL

Problem: The player jabs at the ball on short putts, using a nervous "yip" action.

Result: A putt hit on the low side of the hole.

Goal: To let a good stroke take care of business, instead of trying to steer the ball into the hole.

Watch the tee and you'll train yourself to employ an automatic-pilot putting technique.

Practice Procedure: Place a tee in the vent hole of your putter's grip.

Concentrate on the tee at address and keep concentrating on it during the stroke. Johnny Miller focuses on a dot painted on the tip of the grip, which you may like better. In any case, focusing on the tee or the dot, and not the ball, allows you to alleviate anxiety and thus make a smooth, even stroke without thinking about it. I learned this through practice, as have other top tour pros who wanted to cure putting problems.

Take your eyes off the dot when you hear the ball ring in the cup.

RIGHT-ARM TOSS DRILL

Problem: The player's right shoulder and right arm jut outward at the start of the downswing, causing the club to be pulled across the ball.

Result: A slice or a severe pull.

Goal: To employ the correct right-arm, right-shoulder movements, so that you come into the ball from the inside instead of the outside, and hit straight shots rather than slices.

Practice Procedure: The following drill **(see color insert page 1)**, taught to me by former Masters and PGA champion Jack Burke, Jr., will allow you to accomplish your main goal. It also offers the added benefit of helping you learn to properly sequence lower-body action with the correct throwing motion during the swing.

Grip the club in your right hand only. Take your address position, then look down the fairway and pick out a specific target.

Swing the club back to the three-quarter position.

Start the downswing by taking a small step forward with your left foot, then actually throw the club on a line drive at the target using an underhand/sidearm throwing motion.

Chapter 2

HOME-SCHOOLING

- *Drills you can do at home to help increase your strength and flexibility*

In the past, an athletically conscious professional golfer like Gary Player was an exception on the PGA Tour. Now, success on the tour goes hand and hand with athleticism. In fact, since a very fit and flexible pro by the name of Tiger Woods emerged on the scene in 1996—and won the Masters a year later by twelve shots—an increasing number of pro and amateur golfers have started working out regularly. You should, too.

The stronger and more flexible your body, the more able you'll be to employ the body action we all teach at the Jim McLean Golf School. Furthermore, you will turn your body more powerfully and thus hit the ball longer off the tee, from fairway grass, and out of heavy rough. For these reasons, I devote this chapter to stretching and strengthening drills that can be done in the privacy of your home or backyard.

My great friend and veteran golf teacher Carl Welty proved to me many years ago that a tremendous amount of golf swing improvement could be done away from the golf course. Therefore, at each of my golf school locations, instructors teach students to take the training process home with them. We have our students hit balls into a net at our super-stations and show them how to practice indoors.

Follow in the footsteps of the top pros who partake in at-home exercise programs. There is this added bonus: Regular workouts teach you to be more self-disciplined and determined. These plus-factors, together with the strong sense of confidence you will gain, will help you achieve your golf goals much more quickly.

STRETCHING DRILLS

TORSO-TWIST DRILL *(Timeless Winner)*

Problem: The golfer's coiling action on the backswing and uncoiling action on the downswing are weak and not very rhythmic.

Result: This problem leads to a loss of power in the swing and also a loss of distance, particularly off the tee.

Goal: To find a drill that will help you coil and uncoil your body to the max and enhance the balance and rhythm of your swing motion.

The Torso-Twist Drill will help you strengthen your body coil and uncoil actions.

Practice Procedure: Start out by doing this exercise—which I learned from observing Jack Nicklaus—for one minute, or about ten repetitions in both directions. Later, you can increase the number of repetitions as you slowly increase flexibility and coil.

Take your normal driver address position. Next, place a golf club behind your back and hold it in the crooks of your arms. Next, squeeze or tighten your abdominal muscles. Then, while breathing normally, slowly turn your entire torso to the right; hold, then turn your torso slowly but fully to the left. Also, make certain to keep both shoulders back and your spine straight (not slumped), which will enable you to reap the greatest rewards.

SWING A WEIGHTED DRIVER

Problem: The player fails to make a good weight-shift action on both the backswing and downswing, and needs to increase his or her flexibility.

Result: Loss of vital power in the swing.

Goal: To find an exercise drill that forces the shift and re-shift action to be exaggerated, so that their feel makes a deep impression. The more you feel those weight-shifting actions, the more likely you will be to pivot onto your right foot and leg on the backswing, and your left foot and leg on the downswing.

Swinging a weighted club back and through will enhance your pivot actions.

Practice Procedure: Purchase a special weighted driver from your local golf professional, or use lead tape to load up an old driver out of the garage. Lead tape can also be purchased from your pro, and it's easy to stick onto the driverhead. Make the weight approximately twenty-two ounces.

Next, set up normally. When swinging indoors, make certain the ceiling is high enough to enable you to swing freely.

Swing slowly back, concentrating on employing a full, fluid motion, rather than a fast one. As you slowly move the club into the backswing, you'll feel the weight of the club working on your forearms. Later, after your arms have passed waist height and the clubshaft has passed perpendicular, you'll actually feel it begin to pull on your hips, your back, and your shoulders, so that they'll want to keep turning even farther. Whatever the length of your backswing is currently, the weight of the training club will encourage you to go beyond it and make a much more solid pivot action onto your right side. Just be aware that your weight should not travel to the outside of the back foot, nor should your head slide more than a few inches away from the target.

Start down very slowly and smoothly, letting the extra weight of the club promote a solid shift into your left side.

Gene Sarazen, a winner of all four major championships and someone I played numerous rounds with as a young professional, was the pro that first popularized swinging a weighted club. Sarazen swung the weighted club every day, which is probably why he hit the ball so well when we played. He was in his late seventies when I played with him; he shot par or better every single time we teed it up. He played good golf into his nineties.

Tailoring the Tip: There are now shorter weighted iron clubs that some of our students find more manageable. You may want to consider purchasing one at your local pro shop.

MEDICINE-BALL DRILL

Problem: The player makes the mistake of over-controlling the swing with the smaller muscles in his hands.

Result: This fault causes the player to swing the arms faster, but not powerfully. The reason: He fails to coordinate the body-coil with the arms-swing. More often than not, the club fails to finish square to the ball at impact and the shot flies weakly off-line.

Goal: To discover a drill that trains the bigger muscles of the body to control the swing.

Teacher Jimmy Ballard popularized the Medicine-Ball Drill.

Practice Procedure: Purchase a medicine ball at your local sporting goods store or use a full shag bag. Don't think this is crazy. The great Ben Hogan used to swing a medicine ball and teacher Jimmy Ballard popularized the following drill. Not only did he teach it to pro students such as Curtis Strange and Hal Sutton, he also had his amateur students work with the "big ball."

Swing the medicine ball back, feeling how the muscles in your arms and shoulders—and torso—stretch. Next, swing the ball through, noting how the *big* muscles promote speed and a free release of the ball.

STRENGTHENING DRILLS

DOORWAY DRILL *(Timeless Winner)*

Problem: The player's left side is not strong enough or trained well enough to direct the clubface squarely into the ball at impact on a consistent basis.

Result: The player tends to pull the ball or hit it thin.

Goal: To find a drill that helps you strengthen and train the left side—the left shoulder, left arm, and left hand—to work efficiently, particularly in the impact area.

This Doorway Drill (left) will train the left side to work efficiently in the impact zone (right).

Practice Procedure: Stand in a doorway with your left foot placed approximately one foot ahead of the wall. Now, extend your left arm out to the edge of the wall. Press the back of your left hand against the wall, making sure your left wrist is kept straight (as it should be at impact). Exert pressure against the wall and hold for a count of ten. Check to see that the upper left arm is held snugly against the left side of your body. You should feel pressure in this area as well as visualize the left arm, the left wrist, and the imaginary club forming a straight line. Burn this image into your mind. Then, when practicing in your backyard or indoor practice-net room, hit very small shots, making certain to maintain these critical impact alignments. It will definitely take time to master this drill when hitting a golf ball, but it will certainly pay off big for those who do.

ON-ONE-LEG DRILL

Problem: The player has poor balance and too much lateral motion. Also, he or she fails to uncoil the right hip powerfully at the start of the downswing, namely because the left leg post is weak.

Result: A weak, extra-high shot.

Goal: To learn how to strengthen the left leg, so it becomes a solid post to coil around, and to enhance balance.

Teacher Ernest Jones popularized the On-One-Leg Drill.

Practice Procedure: Hit plastic balls standing on just your left foot, as top teacher David Lee has been having his students do for years.

To modify this drill, I will have a student pull their left foot back and flare the left toe toward the target. The right foot is now on the ground but forward with the right toe turned toward the target as well. Make sure to use a narrow stance, as this setup will effectively do the same thing as the one-leg drill. You will still feel like you're hitting off the left post.

Chapter 3

BODY DRILLS

- *No-club drills designed to help promote proper body positions and ensure a pro-standard swinging action*

In 1987, my good friend and Top 100 teacher David Glenz and I worked together on an instructional video called *Ten Fundamentals of the Modern Golf Swing*. This tape was revolutionary because for the first time ever it included body drills. Since then I have made a point of including body drills in my writings whenever possible.

Surprisingly, even today many amateur golfers who are sticklers for attempting to get club positions just right never reach a high standard because of a failure to get body positions right. Granted, you can play pretty decent golf as a pure "hands player." But unless you improve your body positions and body sequencing, and learn how to correctly work your body center, you will never reach your golf potential.

Because I put such an important emphasis on the role of the body during the swing, I expect my teachers to provide students with pure body drills. Each and every drill brings the student in tune with the proper body pivot actions and body angles involved in a good golf swing.

Just because none of these drills require a golf club, don't underestimate their value. Aside from the positive points I've already mentioned, body drills teach you the feeling of connection in the swing and thus smooth out your tempo, timing, and rhythm, so that when you do put a club in your hands, you'll swing very efficiently with controlled power.

Because keeping the ball in play is a priority of today's tour professionals, it's no wonder that Tiger Woods and many of his contemporaries work on body drills. I think you will be surprised by how much you can accomplish without swinging a club.

POSTURE DRILL

Problem: The player's address position, namely his or her posture or framework, is incorrect. The player either stoops over or stands too erect at address, or other elements of the setup, such as the width of the stance, are not fundamentally sound.

Result: Weak, off-line shots.

Goal: Since how you stand to the ball plays an important role in the outcome of your swing, your goal is to rehearse a good starting position, making good posture a priority.

Practicing this Posture Drill will ultimately improve your swing action.

Practice Procedure: Stand with your feet shoulder-width apart and your arms at your sides—in the military "attention" position. Bring your hands out in front of you and clap them together at thigh height. While keeping your arms and hands in this clapping position, bend from the hips so that you create a twenty- to thirty-degree angle between the legs and the spine. Next, flex your knees and tip your head slightly downward to look at an imaginary ball.

Once you've established a solid golfer's framework, relax your shoulders, arms, and take some nice cleansing breaths. Move your feet inside your golf shoes to avoid tension in the legs. Check to see that you have approximately the width of one hand between your body and hands. Make sure your spine is just slightly tilted away from the target. Repeat until you can lock into a solid setup every time.

HEAD-MOTION DRILL

Problem: The golfer locks his head during the backswing. Many students we see at our schools take literally the old and incorrect advice, "Keep the head still throughout the swing."

Result: When the head remains locked in position, your upper body cannot shift over the inside of your right leg. Instead, you "reverse pivot," leaving most of your body weight on your left side. You succeed in keeping the head still, but fail to make a powerful athletic coil.

Goal: To understand that it is fine for the head to rotate slightly and laterally during the first half of the swing. By doing this, the upper body is able to "load up" over the right side and position the entire body for a powerful downswing delivery.

When doing the Head-Motion Drill, your objective is to swing back, then look up and see your entire head (left). Remember, this is good because you started out with only half your head visible in the mirror (right).

Practice Procedure: Take your normal address in front of a mirror, closer to its left side, so that your head is half in the mirror and half out. Next, cross your arms in front of your chest. Pretend you are looking down at a ball and proceed to make a full shoulder turn, then stop. Now look up into the mirror. If you can see your full head in the mirror, you have made a correct upper-body pivot. If your head has remained where it was at address, or you can't see your head, then you have not coiled behind the ball and probably do not have enough weight on your right side. Let your head move a few inches or let your chin move away from the target to ensure a solid coil action.

LEFT-ARM-BRUSH DRILL

Problem: The golfer's left arm moves quickly across the chest in the take-away, with the shaft going around and behind the player. When the club passes too far inside and across the chest—into the "danger zone"—erratic shots are a virtual given. He or she must reroute the club outward on the downswing, usually swinging the club over the top of the correct inside swing path.

Result: A loop in the swing and a slice or pull, depending on the clubface position at impact.

Step One

Step Two

Goal: To learn to *brush* the left arm lightly up and across the chest, but not too much, during the first half of the backswing, so that the left arm is in position to move up during the second half of the backswing, not around. With the left arm on-plane you will be better able to deliver it into a square impact position.

Practice Procedure: Take your normal address position. Place the back of your left hand against your right elbow. Now, holding your right hand in the address-type position shown, make a backswing, noting the feel of your left arm brushing across your chest, then moving up.

Because this drill prevents you from pulling the left arm in against the chest, you will not be able to suck the left arm in and around the body. This is an exercise I first observed being taught by teacher David Leadbetter.

THE GRAB DRILL *(Timeless Winner)*

Problem: The golfer's overactive hands and wrists lead to a poor backswing position. The wrist is either open ("cupped") or closed ("bowed") at the top.

Result: An off-target shot—anything from a push slice to a hook.

Goal: To learn to make a connected backswing without independent hand and wrist manipulation. The knuckle count on your left hand should remain the same from address to the top of the backswing. Ideally, you should strive for a flat left wrist at the top of the backswing, where the back of the left hand, the top of the left forearm, and the clubface are all in the same alignment.

Practice Procedure: Without a club, grab your left hand/wrist with your right hand. Assume your golf stance and take this position to the top of the backswing. Hold. Repeat.

This drill should help you develop a one-piece backswing action and position the club correctly at the top, so you can deliver the club back to the ball with a square clubface. I learned this drill many years ago when I worked extensively with Peter Jacobsen. It has been a staple drill that Peter has used since his junior days.

The Grab Drill: Address position and at the top.

RIGHT-HAND-LEFT-ARM CONNECTION DRILL

Problem: The golfer fails to release the club properly through impact, due mainly to letting the left arm move too far way from the body, or "disconnect."

Result: An off-target, left-to-right shot.

Goal: At our schools, teachers often see this problem and use this drill to help students feel the left arm connection. You must learn and feel that the key to keeping the left arm "connected" to the body, when hitting golf shots, is the constant rotation of the entire body through impact and into the follow-through. This drill will help you feel how this connection works, as well as how the upper left (leading) arm stays glued to your left side.

Practice Procedure: Assume your address position. Hold your upper left arm with your right hand, as shown. Make sure that the left arm is on top of the pec muscle and not to the side of your body. Rotate your body slowly toward the target while holding the upper part of your left arm against your chest. Feel the left arm and the inside pocket of the left elbow rotating with the left elbow, and remember to mimic this action when swinging on the course. Practice this move and add a very small takeaway, still holding the upper left arm into your body. Repeat until you get the feeling of the body swinging the arms, which is definitely an advanced ball-striker's action. If you can incorporate this wonderful action into your golf swing, it will really make a difference in your shot-making prowess.

Following these two basic steps will train the left arm to stay "connected" to your body.

DEEP-BREATHING DRILL

Problem: The golfer has so many swing thoughts in his head that he freezes over the ball for as much as thirty seconds, makes a tense backswing action, then tries to steer the club into the ball.

Result: A weak slice.

Goal: To make a free, uninhibited swing, with the unconscious mind controlling the action.

One vital step in practicing the Deep-Breathing Drill is to take a deep breath and hold it in during the backswing action.

Practice Procedure: Take your address position, inhaling and exhaling a couple of times very slowly and clearing all swing thoughts from your head. Breathe in through your nose and exhale through your mouth.

Swing back, taking a deep breath in and holding it. Really let the tension out!

Swing down, exhaling as you swing into the complete finish.

Repeat ten times or until you can make a much more natural, tension-free swing.

Once you feel relaxed, take your clear-head mentality to the course, making sure to do your thinking while standing behind the ball, before you set up. Do not try to think your way through the golf swing.

RIGHT-ARM-ONLY ON-CENTER DRILL

Problem: The player fails to coordinate and blend a timed body swing with a fluid and correct arms-swing action.

Result: He fails to deliver the clubface squarely to the ball at impact and hit on-line shots.

Goal: To learn the true meaning of timing in the golf swing and hit good golf shots.

Practice Procedure: The following drill **(see color insert page 2)** is one we use very frequently at our schools, and was a drill I invented along with the X-Factor concept.

Set up with your left forefinger in the center of your chest.

Swing back with your coil and right arm in sync. Let the right arm swing and fold into a right angle, so the elbow moves away from your shoulder while you feel the movement of your body-center in the area of the sternum. The arm and the shoulder coil arrive at the top of the backswing together.

Swing down, concentrating on swinging the right arm down close to the body and coordinating the movement with that of your body center right through into the finish.

SIDEARM DRILL

Problem: The player turns his right hand and right forearm under the left through impact, so that the right palm and underside of the right forearm face the sky. The right shoulder works too high and over the top.

Result: The shot flies extra-high and carries only a short distance, usually missing the target and often falling well to the right.

Goal: To learn how to correctly rotate the right hand and right arm on the downswing and how the right elbow and right shoulder should lower. In order to swing the club from the inside, then down the line, then inside again, the right forearm and hand must rotate counterclockwise over the left forearm and hand.

Mimic the shortstop's throw to first base when practicing the Sidearm Drill.

Practice Procedure: To groove the correct rotation-action involving the right hand and arm, mimic the shortstop's throw to first base by throwing a ball down the range. Use a combination underhand/sidearm action. Do this over and over until you feel as though you can make an accurate line-drive throw. Once you can make this throw, make slow-motion throws without a ball. Notice how the right elbow leads the hand and how the right elbow must come out in front of the right hip. You cannot make a proper throw with the right elbow staying behind the body. Nor can you throw hard if you release too early. You'll notice how much more power you get when you step into a throw and your body rotates toward the target. You'll also learn just how close this throw action mimics the correct moves of the right arm in the golf swing. Take it from Ben Hogan, who believed that the correct swing of a club closely resembles the action of an infielder as he fields a ball and throws it to first base.

Chapter 4

POWER PLOYS

- *Drills designed to add power and speed to your golf swing*

At each and every Jim McLean Golf School—and particularly at the specialized "Power School"—golf instructors work hard on helping students increase their clubhead speed. The reason: Speed is what allows you to hit the ball farther, provided that you, of course, swing the club on the correct path and plane and return it squarely to the ball at impact.

The drills that follow are especially designed to help you generate high clubhead speed and reach your full power potential as a player. Furthermore, they are part of an overall program that guarantees our students will add at least five miles per hour to their existing clubhead speed during the swing. This means twelve and a half yards to your drive.

You probably know already how great it feels to hit a drive long and straight, since even high-handicappers usually hit one powerhouse tee shot per round. My goal, however, is to get you to enjoy this sensation more often. I'll get you to accomplish that goal by teaching you innovative drills, such as the Swing-Under-the-Shaft and Shaft-Under-Foot Drills. All of these drills promise to help you add yards to your shots, because they teach you how to increase your clubhead speed, make solid contact with the ball, and employ a free release of the club.

HIGH-TEE-HEIGHT DRILL

Problem: The player takes divots with his driver. The player tees up the ball lower to compensate for an overly steep swing.

Result: The player's drives fly a short distance and drift right of the target. One thing I do not allow at our schools is taking a divot with your driver. So if you do this, read on carefully.

Goal: To promote a shallow swing arc, a longer flat spot through impact, and more penetrating drives that draw.

Notice that the tee has not moved. That's because I swung the club through on a shallow arc then swept the ball cleanly off the tee.

Practice Procedure: Take your normal setup position for a driver, then tee the ball up very high (at least one inch above the turf). Now replace your driver with a three-metal or five-metal. Next, line up the clubface level with the ball.

Swing back at seventy-five percent of your normal speed. Swing down and through, concentrating on sweeping the ball cleanly off the tee.

This drill will quickly and dramatically show your swing flaws. A miss with the shallow face fairway metals will result in a total pop-up. When working on this drill, you may find that a higher tee height, like that used by Sergio Garcia, is the one that helps you make a stronger wind up of the body, swing on a shallower plane, and hit powerful tee shots.

SWING-UNDER-THE-SHAFT DRILL

Problem: The player takes the club outside the target line and usually up on an overly steep plane.

Result: His swing requires a major correction, or poorly hit shots are a certainty.

Goal: To learn to employ a good backswing that helps promote on-target shots.

Practice Procedure: This drill **(see color insert page 3)** will definitely solve your problems.

Stick a shaft through a range ball basket as the photos in the insert show.

Next, swing the club back under the shaft. Keep rehearsing this action.

Next, swing the club down under the shaft. Keep rehearsing this action.

Once you get a feel for the "under" actions, swing and hit the ball.

BRUSH-THE-BALL-AWAY DRILL

Problem: The player lifts the club up too soon in the takeaway, instead of bringing it back low to the ground for about twelve inches and triggering a wide-arc swing.

Result: Fat iron shots, weak drives.

Goal: To groove a low takeaway action that will ultimately help promote powerfully hit shots.

Practice Procedure: Tee up a ball. Place a tee in the ground approximately twelve inches directly behind the teed up ball. Set up to the ball with a driver. Push the club back, trying to brush the ball off the tee by letting the triangle formed by your arms and shoulders control the action. Now take this sweeping takeaway to the course and watch your shots fly hard off the clubface.

TEE ——→

Practicing brushing the ball off a tee will help you develop a low takeaway action.

LEFT-KNEE DRILL

Problem: The player does not use the lower body. It's what teachers at my schools refer to as *dead legs*. This is because the player fails to use his or her left knee to trigger a rhythmic backswing action. Instead, the player keeps the feet, knees, and hips locked, while exaggerating upper-body action. Or he or she stands up, losing the flex in the knees on the backswing.

Result: A weak, off-line shot, or a "top."

Goal: To find a way to make a smooth transition from address to the backswing and generate power while maintaining your spine angle. You must shift your weight correctly on the backswing and coil into your back leg, so that by the time you reach the top of the swing your weight is loaded on your right foot and leg and your right knee has maintained its flex. Then you will you be ready to unleash the club into the ball.

Practice Procedure: Tee up a ball, using a square stance.

Swing back, concentrating on moving your hands, the club, and your left knee together. Feel pressure off the instep of the left foot. The left knee will gradually break inward and behind the golf ball. You will likely need to practice hard, doing this drill to sync up the upper and lower body properly.

This drill will encourage you to shift your weight to your right side automatically, as well as free up any stiff lower-body action. By pivoting correctly and using better footwork, you will automatically reduce the lifting or dropping of the upper body and employ a much more fluid swing motion. This is another drill that I've used with golfers of every skill level, even top professionals.

Rotating the left knee inward will help you make a smooth transition into the backswing.

RAISE-YOUR-HEEL DRILL

Problem: The golfer is lost as to how to start the swing. The common tendency is to freeze over the ball and then suddenly snatch the club back quickly, usually too far inside the target line. Many golfers just cannot get started, and vary their takeaway action from shot to shot.

Result: Anything from a weak slice to a hook, depending on the player's timing.

Goal: To learn to make a smooth start to the swing and realize that a flowing tempo in the takeaway encourages an overall action that is smooth and controlled.

Practicing this right-foot-lift move may turn your swing problem around.

Practice Procedure: Just before starting the swing, raise your right heel slightly off the ground, so you feel some weight start to shift into your left leg. This is an ignition move to get things in motion.

Next, replant your right foot to trigger a smooth takeaway that allows your body weight to shift into your right leg. This right-heel trigger creates a far more athletic move away from the ball—one that is dynamic rather than static, and that helps you start building power. I say the "first move" in the golf swing is actually toward the target. Watch the tour professionals and see if you can't see the subtle move in every one of them. Actually lifting the right heel can be a slight overkill, so you may end up just feeling a small push forward off the right instep. Yet even great players like Sam Snead did lift the right heel to start the golf swing, but then employed a smooth motion.

BE-LIKE-MOE DRILL

Problem: The golfer hinges the wrists too early on the backswing, causing an overly steep and weak swing, or tends to dip the body.

Result: Fat irons, extra-high woods.

Goal: To learn to create width in the backswing, so in turn you promote a shallow angle of attack and a long flat spot through impact. Also, to maintain your height during the backswing.

Practice Procedure: I played many tournament rounds with Moe Norman, the super-talented Canadian professional, and practiced with him on numerous occasions.

At address, Moe did something unusual. He placed the club twelve inches behind the ball. What this does is give you a "running start" to a correct takeaway, with the wrist remaining unhinged, and also keeps your center up. Your club is basically preset on a perfect path, with the clubface square. All you have to do is put it there and then go. I used this drill very successfully with tour professional Brad Faxon. In fact, that's how I invented this drill for students. Brad tended to overextend and drop center (his sternum) in the backswing. This drill helped immensely.

If setting up with the club this far behind the ball works for Moe Norman, it may work for you.

BALLARD LOGO DRILL *(Timeless Winner)*

Problem: The golfer's arms outrace the turn of the body.

Result: When your timing is off, power is drained from the swing and accurate shots are not in the cards.

Goal: To synchronize the arms and body in the first part of the backswing.

The triangle formed by your arms and shoulders must stay intact until approximately three feet into the backswing, when the butt end of the club is between your arms and pointing at your midsection. This unification creates a smooth start to the swing and gives the upper body time to turn and load up over the right leg.

Practice Procedure: Address a ball, positioning it opposite the logo on the left breast side of your shirt.

Take the club away in one piece, moving the clubshaft and logo in unison. The left arm should not cross over the logo.

This drill, devised by instructor Jimmy Ballard, is great for grooving a smooth, one-piece takeaway with the arms and the upper body moving in unison.

When working on the Ballard Logo Drill, the logo should be visible as the takeaway action is employed.

POSITION-YOUR-BACKSWING DRILL

Problem: The golfer does not have any concept of where the hands, arms, and clubhead should be at the top of the backswing. Therefore, he or she sometimes makes too long or too short of a backswing, or swings the club back on either an overly flat or overly upright plane.

Result: Just about any kind of poorly hit shot is possible.

Goal: To know and feel a correct at-the-top position, so that you can consistently deliver the club squarely into the ball at impact.

Position-Your-
Backswing Drill:
Look and learn.

Practice Procedure: Take your address position, gripping the club in your normal manner. Raise the club up in front of you to waist height. Next, cock your wrists directly toward your right shoulder area until the shaft is pointing skyward. Now lay the shaft on the top of your right shoulder. Turn your shoulders ninety degrees to the target, with your back to the hole and your left shoulder positioned over the inside of your right leg. Last, push your hands straight away and up from your right shoulder and parallel to the target line.

Practice this drill at home (ideally, in front of a mirror) and program the feel of where the backswing should end up, then incorporate it into your swing. You can even hit balls on the range using this position drill. Students are often totally amazed at the positive results.

TEE-IN-GRIP DRILL

Problem: The golfer's overactive, improper use of the hands causes the club-head to rotate dramatically over and well inside the target line. In turn, the golfer's arms and body are not in sync.

Result: In order to hit a powerful shot, he or she must rely on some kind of miraculous manipulation with the hands. The chances of success: slim and none.

Goal: To learn to blend body movement with the actions of the hands and arms. When these factors are in sync, no mid-swing compensations are needed, and a repeatable good swing is easier to attain.

Practicing the Tee-in-Grip Drill will teach you to keep your distance during the swing.

Practice Procedure: Using a five-iron or longer club, place a tee peg in the vent hole of the grip. Choke down on the grip slightly. Now, make a very short mini-backswing, keeping the distance between the tee and your belt buckle constant. You should feel zero hand action.

Practicing this drill a couple of times a day for about a week will allow you to calm the hands and be positioned to make a technically sound, well-timed downswing.

RIGHT-ELBOW-CORRECTION DRILL

Problem: On the backswing, the player keeps the right elbow tucked in too close to the body or, more commonly, lets it fly too far outward on the downswing.

Result: Either movement is a swing fault. Either fault will usually lead to a weak, off-line shot.

Goal: To learn to let the right arm and right elbow form an L-shape at the top of the swing. The upper-left arm should be nearly parallel to the shaft-plane line, upper-left the right forearm pointing toward the target.

Practice Procedure: Keep your left arm behind your back when taking your stance. Swing the right arm and club back, allowing the right elbow to fold naturally. Repeat this motion until you can successfully arrive at a solid backswing position with the clubshaft pointed toward the target and the right arm forming the L-position. You might feel like a waiter carrying an imaginary tray in his right hand, which is an old but reliable image that top teachers, including Phil Ritson and Hank Haney, have used with their students for a long time.

When practicing the Right-Elbow-Correction Drill, you should feel like a waiter carrying a tray when you reach the top of the swing.

SWING-PLANE DRILL

Problem: The golfer swings the club on an incorrect plane.

Result: This fault prevents him or her from making square and solid contact with the ball.

Goal: To learn to swing the club on the correct orbital path, so that you are positioned to hit powerfully accurate shots.

Practice Procedure: Place two shafts on the ground to represent the target line and two tees outside the target line. Stick a tee in the grip end of the club before setting up.

Start the backswing. As you swing back to the three-quarter position, the tee in the grip of the club should point at the target line or out to the tee line. If the butt of the club points well past or over the target line, the plane angle is too flat, and you need to do further work. But stay with this drill. It works wonders!

When working on the Swing-Plane Drill, make sure the tee points near the target line as you swing the club back.

SQUARE-CLUBFACE DRILL

Problem: The player swings the club back either into an extremely open or closed position during the backswing. If the toe of the clubhead points straight down on the backswing, the clubface is excessively closed and is likely to be that way at impact. If the clubface points directly upward at the sky on the backswing, it is open and will likely return to that position at impact.

Result: The open clubface fault will usually cause a slice, while the closed clubface position will probably result in a hook.

Goal: To swing the club back to a square position at the top, so that returning it to a square impact position—a link to power—requires no manipulation of the club with the hands.

The Square-Clubface Drill in pictures: Look and learn.

Practice Procedure: Take your address position, with the clubface square to the target. Swing the club halfway back, consciously thinking about working the clubhead into a toe-up position. If you turn your body to face the club and then drop the clubhead straight down it will still be dead square, as one of my mentors, U.S. Open champion Ken Venturi, showed me when he taught me this drill. Just knowing that when the toe of the club points up at the sky it means the clubface is square will help you employ the right physical movements to make this happen. If you practice this drill thinking "hand back of the clubhead" and then "turn to the top," you will quickly learn what your hands, arms, and shoulders must do to swing the club back to a square position. The added bonus: You will take the bad angles out of your swing.

POWER-COIL DRILL *(Timeless Winner)*

Problem: The backswing turning action of the shoulders is weak. A weak turn also plays havoc with the weight shift action when swinging back, and it also usually causes an incorrect downswing sequence, with the upper body rather than the lower body leading the way.

Result: The player fails to generate power in the swing.

Goal: To build a strong backswing shoulder-turning action.

Step One

Step Two.

Practice Procedure: Take your normal driver stance and posture, then hold a clubshaft in front of and across your shoulders. Next, place a second clubshaft on the ground, so that it extends outward from approximately your right heel and runs perpendicular to an imaginary target line.

Now swing back a few times, making sure to rotate your shoulders enough to allow the "high" shaft to pass the "low" shaft until both shafts are virtually parallel to one another. This will ensure that you have coiled powerfully behind the golf ball. Make sure to stay level. Do not raise your head. Do not move your head excessively away from the target. Keep your eyes on an imaginary ball.

Eventually, this drill can be done on the range when hitting balls, using just the shaft running off the inside of the right heel. This is a great power-producing drill. The more you practice this drill, the stronger your shoulder turn will become. When you return to the course, you'll hit the ball much more powerfully—guaranteed.

SHAFT-UNDER-FOOT DRILL

Problem: The player turns the hips too much, destroying the resistance between the upper and lower body. He or she does not understand my "X-Factor" power coil, which explains how the shoulders should turn far more than the hips.

Result: A weak shot.

Goal: To produce power, the player must learn that you have to increase what I call the X-Factor differential between the shoulder and hip turns. To get a feel for the proper amount of hip turn, work on the following drill.

Swinging with the grip end of a club under your right foot will train you to make the correct degree of hip turn.

Practice Procedure: Place the grip end of a shaft under the outside of your right foot. Swing back. The wedge you built under your shoe puts a governor on your right hip, so you learn not to over-turn it. You might also try boxing the right toe inward, if—and only if—you can still make a full shoulder turn. When you swing, you will turn your shoulders much more than your hips and achieve a high X-Factor rating. You will also really stabilize the right leg.

Keep practicing until you turn correctly and begin hitting powerful shots. You can hit balls with this drill with no problem.

L–SWING DRILL

Problem: The "L"s formed by the left arm and clubshaft are not maintained early in the backswing, nor on the way down.

Result: The player cannot return the clubface squarely to the ball and generate adequate power. I've used this idea of the letter "L" in previous books, because it presents a very clear image to the student and thus promotes good results.

Goal: To concentrate on your Ls and learn to make square and solid contact with the ball.

Be conscious of your Ls as you practice swinging.

Practice Procedure: Swing back, being very conscious of creating a pure L. If you feel you're off, have a friend shape the L, then stop and feel that good backswing position for a few seconds.

Swing down slowly, maintaining the L by returning the hinge in your right wrist.

Rehearse these key positions, practicing them over and over. Next, swing through these two key positions going back to the top and through to the finish. Now you're ready to hit balls and experience the feeling of solidly hitting on-target shots.

LEFT-HIP DRILL

Problem: The player exaggerates leg drive to such a degree that the left hip fails to clear, or he swings on an exaggerated inside-out path.

Result: The player is blocked from returning the club squarely and solidly to the ball.

Goal: To time the downswing better and learn how to rotate the left hip to the left through impact, such that high clubhead speed and power are a virtual "lock."

Practice Procedure: Take your setup. Next, have a friend place an old clubshaft in the ground, about two inches in front of the outside of your left foot. Also, angle the shaft back to allow for free hip clearing.

Swing back normally.

Start down. Once you make a solid weight shift into your left side, rotate your left hip in time to avoid the shaft. If your hip touches the shaft, you know you have to work harder on this drill to tame your lateral leg drive. You'll also finish in a more upright, balanced position, which is much easier on the back.

Tom Kite, the 1992 U.S. Open champion, used this drill extensively to improve his swing speed and gain distance off the tee prior to winning that Open. I still use this drill even when working with Tom to this day.

When practicing the Left-Hip Drill, the objective is to rotate your left hip away from the shaft in the ground.

IN-THE-SLOT DRILL

Problem: The player releases the right wrist and/or right elbow much too early in the downswing.

Result: "Casting" the club like this is a direct cause of a weak, misdirected shot.

Goal: To learn to maintain the hinge in the right wrist and right elbow until you reach the impact zone. When you "delay the hit," as teachers say, you preserve power until the impact zone, when the club is whipped into and then through the ball at high speed.

Practice Procedure: Assume a powerful stance—one that has the proper golfer's framework and solid balance.

Swing to the top and hold that position for a few seconds.

Start unwinding your hips on the downswing. Simultaneously, drop your right elbow down in front of your right hip, then freeze this position. Feel the arms fall and do not uncock the wrists. This move trains your right wrist to remain cocked and teaches you to feel the sensation of delaying the hit, without feeling the need to pull on the butt end of the club.

In practice, "freeze" this proper right elbow position and you'll put the club in the slot every time.

LET-GO DRILL

Problem: The player either lets the left arm "break down," overuses the right hand to control the downswing action, or fails to follow through fully.

Result: The player usually hits a duck hook that does not fly very far.

Goal: To intellectually appreciate and physically feel a free swing action and continuation of the left arm.

If you think an overactive right hand is your problem, try the following drill that I learned from a great Northwest golf teacher named Harry Umbinetti. It's a drill I also use to help keep students from quitting on their shots.

Let go with your right hand and let the left arm bring the club through impact and into the finish.

Practice Procedure: Tee up every shot.

Swing back to the top, using a seven-iron.

As you swing through, let go of the club with your right hand. The club will fly through the impact zone and the left arm will continue to a full finish. You simply cannot stop.

Repeat this drill until you feel you've tamed the right hand, trained the left arm to keep moving, and are finishing fully on every shot.

Next, hit balls. You should immediately feel how doing drill-work enabled you to restore equality back to the hands and to literally "let go." When you hit shots, the left hand will lead the club into impact, and you'll be amazed at how far you can launch the ball down the fairway with just the left arm finishing the shot.

RELEASE-LOW-AND-THROUGH DRILL

Problem: The golfer hangs back on his or her right side through impact and the right shoulder dips downward dramatically. The golfer's right hand then turns under the left, causing the club's effective loft to be increased at impact.

Result: A weak, extra-high shot. Or, if the golfer hangs back and flips the clubhead, a snap-hook.

Goal: To learn to make a solid shift into the left leg post, then drive a squared-up clubface through impact in a more streamlined fashion.

Practice Procedure: Take a seven-iron in your right hand only and choke down several inches on the grip. Address the ball with your normal setup. Hit teed up balls with your right arm only. You will quickly see that your right shoulder must drive forward toward the ball, rotate, and stay virtually level through impact. When you successfully hit right-arm-only shots, begin hitting two-armed shots, concentrating on making the right shoulder finish more low and around.

Hitting shots with your right hand only will help promote the proper weight-shift action and right-shoulder movements involved in the swing.

SWISH DRILL

Problem: The player prematurely releases the club.

Result: Power is drained from the swing and the trajectory of the shot is off.

Goal: To learn how to better time the downswing action, so that power is preserved for the vital moment of impact.

Practice Procedure: Turn your driver upside down or, better yet, use a driver shaft with no clubhead. If you use your regular driver, grip the shaft directly below the clubhead. Take your address and then swing. If you hear a swish sound right away while swinging down, you have released the club too early. This fault is called "casting."

Swing the club several more times, paying particular attention to the downswing action. Concentrate on maintaining your wrist hinge so that you hear the swish sound later in the downswing.

Now hit shots. You'll see the ball fly lower, farther, and straighter.

When practicing the
Swish Drill, it's
important to delay
the release on the
downswing.

TWO-CLUB DRILL

Problem: The golfer has trouble synchronizing the arms and body and, as a result, the timing of his or her swing is thrown off.

Result: Power is drained from the swing and shots finish short of the player's intended target.

Goal: To learn to better time and coordinate arm action with body action.

This drill will enhance the timing of your swing action.

Practice Procedure: This drill may not allow you to swing as smoothly as Sam Snead did during his heyday, but it will sure help you to iron out your timing problems.

Place a five-iron in one hand and a six-iron in the other. Assume your setup position.

Swing both clubs up to the top simultaneously, trying to keep them the same distance apart. At first, this will likely feel quite awkward, so you'll probably need numerous repetitions to feel comfortable. However, once you can accomplish this goal, make full swings, back and forth, swinging the clubs together in perfect time.

One of my old friends, Floyd Horgen, has used this drill for twenty years or more, and it once helped PGA Tour player Hal Sutton come out of a slump in the early 1990s. It's truly a terrific drill for coordinating your arms and the feel of equal balance in your swing, and with that, to regain lost power.

CHAIR DRILL

Problem: The amateur player's problem is very similar to one that my professional student Len Mattiace once experienced. He moved his hips so vigorously on the downswing that he "lost his spine angle," as we teachers say.

Result: Power leaks from the swing.

Goal: To learn to remain tilted and balanced and slow down the hips, so maximum clubhead speed can be applied to the ball at impact.

The Chair Drill in pictures:
Look and learn.

Practice Procedure: Here's the drill I used to solve Lenny's problem.

Get into your setup and have someone slide a chair up against your back hip pockets.

On the backswing, feel your right hip pocket stay against the chair. It should not move inward, away from the chair, which would indicate that you're either standing up or shifting your weight toward the toes (spine-angle problems).

On the forward swing, as you come into impact, keep pressure against the chair. This was the problem Len had with his forward swing. He moved his hips inward, which caused his spine to rise up slightly. In turn, this caused the club to approach from too steep an angle and too much from the inside. This drill really helped Len stay in his spin angle and to become a consistent tour player and two-time winner. It will help you hit the ball more powerfully on a consistent basis, and thus make you a tougher competitor, too.

 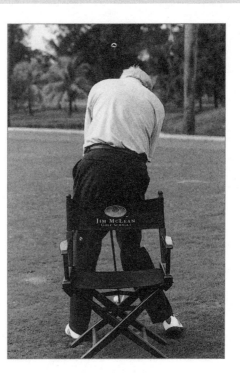

POWER-EXTENSION DRILL

Problem: The player fails to employ good arm-club extension in the takeaway and/or follow-through.

Result: The player fails to create a wide and powerful swing arc.

Goal: To learn how to stay down and through during the swing and produce more powerful shots via solid extension.

Practice Procedure: Take your golf posture with your hip pockets against a wall and your body parallel to the wall, especially your shoulders. Now, hold a beach ball or Swiss ball between your hands in a fully extended setup position, palms facing each other.

Next, swing the ball back, maintaining the triangle formed by your shoulders, arms, and hands that have hold of the ball. Do not let the triangle break down. Your right arm should finish flat against the wall. Hold this ideal position for five seconds.

Now swing the arms and body through to the other side. You can allow the hips to turn slightly, but keep your head very steady. There should be very little drift of the head and virtually no up and down motion. Of course, your head must swivel on the finish, moving as if your ear were resting on a pillow. Make sure to keep the triangle intact all the way.

Tailoring the Tip: Another tip is to use your feet and hips as you move to the halfway finish position. You should pump your feet (shift your weight while exerting pressure) and turn the left hip. My good friend from Australia, Ramsay McMaster, showed me this drill. Ramsey runs the fitness program for the Victorian Institute of Sport.

This is a great drill for feeling "extension" and the movements of an imaginary triangle during the swing.

FOOTWORK DRILL

Problem: The golfer lifts his or her left heel in the backswing, which is okay, but then instead of replanting it in the same position, he or she replants it closer to the right foot. Surprisingly, players who keep their left heel planted during the backswing can still back their left heel up during the downswing. When this move occurs, too much of the player's weight stays on the back leg at impact, which almost always causes him or her to spin the hips.

Result: Typically a weak shot, usually a slice.

Goal: To incorporate good footwork into the swing, so that more power can be generated.

When doing the Footwork Drill, the objective is to keep a second ball touching your left heel.

Practice Procedure: Grip a seven-iron and take your stance. Next, drag another ball up against your left heel. Now, take your full setup.

Make a three-quarter backswing.

Swing down, trying to hit the ball you addressed without the ball by your left heel moving. If the ball by your left heel moves, your weight has shifted incorrectly on the downswing. When you can hit shots without this ball moving, you will see dramatic improvements in your ball-striking, both with metal woods and irons.

ROLL-THE-FEET DRILL

Problem: The player's front knee over-rotates on the backswing, and the back knee slides toward the front knee on the downswing.

Result: The entire shift and rotate action is thrown out of sync, causing the player to mishit the ball.

Goal: To learn proper knee action, which makes for solid shift and re-shift actions and powerful shots.

As you swing back (left), be conscious of rolling off the instep of your front foot. As you swing down (right), be conscious of pushing off your right foot and rolling weight onto your left foot.

Practice Procedure: Establish a comfortably correct address position, so you feel slight pressure on the inside muscles of your feet and legs and your weight is balanced, fifty percent on each foot.

Next, begin the motion by rolling off the instep of your front foot. At the same time, the front knee will move in the same direction, but not too much. This is what you want. Just make sure your back foot and leg can accept the weight transfer without swaying. That means not having the weight transfer to the outside of your back foot.

Next, reverse direction. You should feel pressure off the instep of your back foot. This is a move that ignites the change of direction, proving that golf is played from the "ground up," to borrow a phrase from the late Claude Harmon, Sr. The back knee kicks out at the golf ball and does not slide at the front knee.

When practicing this drill, weight should transfer first to the ball of the front foot, but as the hips turn toward the target, weight should naturally work toward the heel of the front foot. Also, you want to finish on a flat or stable front foot.

Repeat this drill over and over. Gradually, you will synchronize everything. You will also gain a great feel and rhythm in your feet. You will sense when you are stuck to the ground, and conversely when you are moving too fast.

HEAD-STILL DRILL

Problem: The head moves off the ball excessively. This fault causes the player to make such a violent sway away from the target that, ultimately, he or she can do little else but leave a great degree of weight on the right side during the downswing.

Result: An exaggerated hang-back-and-hit move that usually results in a weak slice.

Goal: To control head motion, so that only natural rotation occurs.

Practice Procedure: I learned the following drill from former Masters champion George Archer, who practiced it quite frequently on the range.

Place a broken shaft in the ground about one foot out past the ball, but directly on line with your nose. Angle the shaft so that it points directly at your head, but doesn't interfere with your swing.

Practice your backswing, keeping your eyes on the end of the shaft. It will be very easy to detect any sideways head motion.

Once you eliminate excessive head movement, hit balls, again focusing on the shaft in the ground.

Tailoring the Tip: Since some players reverse pivot—that is, they tilt their head and upper body toward the target on the backswing—I recommend that they practice the same shaft drill. If this is your problem, actually try to move your head laterally several inches to break your bad habit. Once you do, go back and monitor head movement using the original George Archer drill.

When working on the Head-Still Drill and swinging back, keep your eyes on the shaft in the ground, as I do here.

IMPACT DRILL

Problem: Poor clubface control, particularly at impact.

Result: The player hits a garden variety of shots right of the target.

Goal: To understand the impact position, both physically and intellectually, so that square impact to the ball can be made consistently.

The unique thing about the Impact Drill is that you start at impact (left) and end in the finish position (right). You also actually hit the ball.

Practice Procedure: Start at impact. In short, simulate the perfect impact position. This includes putting seventy-five percent of your weight on the front foot, turning the hips left, flattening the left wrist, lifting the right heel off the ground, and setting the left shoulder much higher than the right. I suggest cutting out a picture of your favorite tour professional to study, or using the accompanying photograph as a model.

From your "impact start," take the club away and hit shots. At first, this will feel awkward, but in a short time you'll get the hang of it. This simulation drill can absolutely give you a totally different understanding of where you need to be as you strike the golf ball. I first saw this drill used by legendary teacher and player Bob Toski.

DELAY DRILL

Problem: The player releases the club too early.

Result: This fault causes a loss of clubhead speed and, ultimately, a loss of power.

Goal: To discover a way to feel the proper action of the delayed hit via a simple drill, then incorporate this movement into your swing.

The Delay Drill is very unique, but it really teaches you the ins and outs of a delayed-hit action.

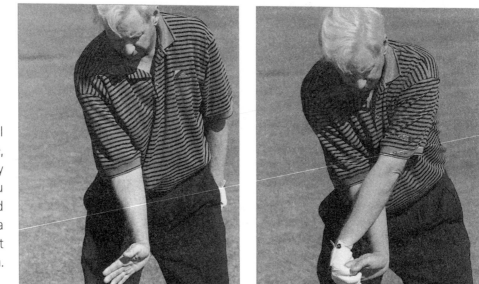

Practice Procedure: Cock the right wrist back. Actually bend it back away from the target. Most people can create almost a forty-five-degree angle. Next, use the left hand to pull your fingers back more, so you maintain the wrist cock throughout the drill.

Now swing your arms back to the three-quarter position. Hold this position and then begin to move the left arm toward impact, all the time holding that angle of the right wrist. As you do this, notice how the right elbow moves out in front of your right hip. Again, hold this pre-impact position for just a moment.

Now release the left hand grip on those fingers and feel the snap of the right arm and right wrist through the impact zone. You can even allow both arms to release to a full finish.

This drill not only gives you an excellent sense of delay, it puts the right arm in a powerful delivery position. After you get the feel of this drill, hit some balls. Go back to the drill between shots, all the while striving for the feel of delay in your swing.

BASKETBALL DRILL

Problem: The player fails to create power on the backswing because he or she doesn't do what great players, namely Ben Hogan and Tiger Woods, have always stressed: Build lower-body resistance.

Result: Shots finish well short of the intended target.

Goal: To maximize resistance in the golf swing and hit the ball with controlled power.

The Basketball Drill is designed to help you learn how to resist with the lower body on the backswing and not over-coil the hips.

Practice Procedure: I first saw teacher Irv Schloss use this drill many years ago. Irv used a basketball, while David Leadbetter and other modern-day teachers use a beach ball to illustrate resistance in the backswing with the lower body.

To stop overactive knee action and learn to feel lower-body resistance, swing back keeping a ball between your knees. If the ball drops out, you know you either over-rotated your hips in a clockwise direction or straightened your right leg.

Practice until you can make a full backswing coil, holding the ball in place.

Bring this ball image to the course, and you'll notice a big difference in how far you hit the ball.

KNEEL-DOWN-SWING DRILL

Problem: The player exaggerates body action in the swing, swaying the lower body on the backswing and employing a leg-lunging action on the downswing.

Result: Severely inconsistent shots.

Goal: To learn how to calm the lower body and depend on a fluid arm swing to achieve square and solid clubface-to-ball contact.

Practice Procedure: You'll find this drill (**see color insert page 4**) a real challenge and get a real kick out of practicing it.

Tee up a ball. Kneel down on a towel, giving yourself ample room to extend your arms, and set the clubface squarely to the ball.

Swing back, feeling active arm action and calmer lower-body action.

Swing down and through, concentrating on how the arms swing the club through the ball.

SHAFT-REGULATOR DRILL

Problem: The player exhibits poor leg action, straightening his or her right leg early in the backswing, or sways the body.

Result: These faults are a hindrance to balance and body coil during the swing and prevent the player from hitting the ball powerfully.

Goal: To establish and maintain the proper flex of the right leg during the swing, in order to create and release power.

When working on the Shaft-Regulator Drill, the angle of the clubshaft must remain constant from address to the top of backswing.

Practice Procedure: Here is a very simple drill that one of my teachers, Tommie Marino, has had great success using at my schools, primarily because it gives the student immediate feedback and positive results. This drill is multifunctional and is great for kids.

While standing in front of a mirror, place the clubface of a pitching wedge underneath your back foot so you sense light pressure on the inside of your back leg.

Swing back. Look at the angle of the shaft. If the shaft's angle goes unchanged, your leg and body actions are good. If the shaft begins to drop, you have straightened the right leg and swayed. Practice this drill until you can swing back, with the shaft staying at its natural launch angle.

MADE-TO-MEASURE DRILL

Problem: The player changes his or her ball position and distance from the ball. On good days, he or she positions the ball off the left heel, allowing for plenty of room to swing. On bad days, he or she plays the ball in the middle of the stance, which is okay for short irons, but not drives. Additionally, he or she "crowds" the ball.

Result: The player hits the ball powerfully one weekend, then hits weak tee shots the next, even though it feels as though he or she is making the same swing.

Goal: To find a way to groove the same ball position by working on a drill, and in the process develop a system for long-term power hitting.

Practice Procedure: The next time you hit the ball great, take a tape measure out of your bag and have a friend measure the distance from your left heel back to the ball, then from the center of the ball back to an imaginary line running across your toes.

Once you have your measurements, when you return to the course the next weekend, take out your ruler on the practice tee when hitting balls before play. Set up according to your calculations, then hit balls. You'll probably see that you hit it great more often, just like you did the previous weekend. You are now ready to do battle with the course.

Tailoring the Tip: Instead of using a ruler, you can use one of the clubs in your bag to act as a measuring tool. Your eight-iron will work perfectly, if you measure from the bottom of the grip to the ball.

In practice, it's a good idea to check if your setup "measures" up.

Chapter 5
WORKING THE BALL

- *Drills that will help you learn how to curve the ball left or right and control its trajectory*

If you go through golf's record books, noting the most frequent major championship winners, you'll notice that they all possess the ability to work the ball.

I accept the fact that Jack Nicklaus, the leading major championship winner, relied mostly on his bread-and-butter fade, as did Ben Hogan before him. However, it's also true that they, like Tiger Woods, hit an array of other shots, knowing how handy different shots are when you want to do such things as cut a dogleg, cheat the wind, hit around trouble, or stop the ball quickly on a hard and fast putting surface.

I've included this chapter not to try to turn you into a shot-making virtuoso, but rather to increase your repertoire of shots enough to make a difference in your scoring.

What I think you will like about the instruction is its simplicity. Instead of teaching you the numerous swing keys necessary for hitting each creative shot, I simply provide you with drills that will teach you to evolve into a shot-maker much more quickly and naturally. That's a promise, and I'll make one more: Once you complete this chapter and practice the various drills, you'll actually welcome a course situation that calls for you to work the ball left, right, high, or low.

DRAW DRILL #1

Problem: The player does not understand the feeling of the proper release action needed to draw the ball. Therefore, he or she lacks the ability to hit a controlled draw (or hook) around a dogleg-left hole, or around trees when playing a recovery shot with an iron. Also, he or she cannot manage the low draw to a back left pin.

Result: The player exaggerates the release dramatically and ends up hitting a duck hook rather than a controlled draw.

Goal: To learn how to properly rotate the forearms and clubhead through impact to impart draw-spin on the ball.

Mimicking a tennis player's topspin-forehand technique will help you learn how to hit a draw.

Practice Procedure: Hold a tennis racket in your right hand.

Swing to the halfway-back position.

Start making a forward transition, mimicking the action a tennis player uses when hitting a topspin-forehand shot. Once you feel comfortable, and feel you've learned how to employ the proper counterclockwise rotating action involving the right forearm, hit shots with your right hand only. Finally, hit two-handed golf shots. You're on your way to being cured!

DRAW DRILL #2

Problem: The player is unable to hit a draw because he or she has not learned to deliver the club from the inside.

Result: The player comes into impact from outside the target line, hitting either a pull or a pull-slice.

Goal: To feel the proper inside motion that you need to repeat in order to hit a draw.

Practice Procedure: Place golf balls on the ground in an arc (**see color insert page 5**). I often do this in clinics to vividly demonstrate how the golf club must work in a solid and proper golf swing. In fact, once you set up as illustrated it will be very clear that the clubhead must approach the intended golf ball from the inside.

Place your intended golf ball just inside the arc. Next, swing the club back and then through, inside the ball-line. This is just what the doctor ordered for a slice-hitter looking to hit a draw.

HIGH-SHOT DRILL

Problem: The player does not know how to stay behind the ball through impact, and therefore cannot loft the ball high into the air, particularly when trying to hit over trees. Instead, the player gets out ahead of the ball through impact, finishing with the hands well ahead of the ball.

Result: The player hits a low shot that fails to carry the trees up ahead.

Goal: To learn the sensations of staying behind the ball through impact and making an upswing hit—two keys for playing the high shot.

Practice Procedure: Hit balls off an uphill lie. This drill instantly teaches you to feel the proper swing sensations that increase the effective loft of the club and allow you to hit the ball higher. Make sure to start from a setup that uses the hill to set your front shoulder high and your back shoulder low.

Hitting shots off uphill lies will teach you to stay behind the ball through impact, a vital key to hitting high shots.

FADE DRILL

Problem: The player does know how to properly use his or her left hand and arm in order to hit a fade shot. Therefore, he or she is unable to hit a fade off the tee, or on approach shots when hitting to a hole tucked behind a bunker and located in the front right portion of the green.

Result: The player lets the left hand and wrist break down through impact and hits a shot left of target.

Goal: To learn how to hit a controlled left-to-right shot.

Practice swinging like this to get the feeling of the technique involved in hitting a fade.

Practice Procedure: Since the left hand is the main control hand for the fade, practice swinging a medium iron downward until you get the feeling of holding on to the club slightly more firmly with the left hand, then swing slightly across the target line, holding the clubface open slightly. Think of the technique as a larger version of the one used to hit a soft cut with a Ping-Pong paddle.

LOW-SHOT DRILL

Problem: The player does not know how to keep the ball down when hitting into the wind.

Result: He or she loses distance off the tee and misses greens on approach shots in windy conditions.

Goal: To learn how to hit low, wind-piercing shots.

Practice Procedure: Hit shots off downhill lies, since "chasing" the ball through impact is critical to hitting a low windcheater off a tee or a level lie. Start with a small swing using a seven iron. Try to take a small divot after impact. At first, most people hit behind the ball, so this drill is a real eye-opener. Once you can consistently make solid contact, increase the length of your swings. You will notice the low ball flight and the easy transfer of weight to the left side. Also, don't be surprised if after impact you are "walking" down the hill.

Hitting shots off
downhill lies will teach
you to chase the ball
through impact, a vital
key to hitting the ball
low.

Chapter 6

SURE WAYS TO PERFECT YOUR PITCHING GAME

- *Drills to help you hit good pitch shots*

One of the most fascinating things about golf is how Player A and Player B can both share the same handicap, yet Player A hits the ball an average of fifty yards longer than Player B. One way that Player B keeps up with Player A—scorewise—is by outplaying him with the pitching clubs.

The reason Player B is so much better at pitching the ball has more to do with a hard-work ethic than with any innate abilities. Golfers who possess exceptional pitching skills spend time practicing this shot from different distances and different lies.

If you are like most golfers, you probably spend more time beating balls at the range than practicing pitching. Well, that's a big mistake, since the effective pitch is one of golf's chief stroke-savers.

I understand that you might naturally view pitching practice as a "snooze," so I've devised a number of drills that will help you accelerate the learning process and, because they're so challenging, should keep you amused while being educated.

Let me start your pitching course by showing you the Circle Drill, a proven "timeless winner."

CIRCLE DRILL *(Timeless Winner)*

Problem: The golfer fails to realize the importance of air-time versus roll-time on short pitch shots.

Result: He or she has trouble gauging distance.

Goal: To lean how to determine where to land the ball and how to encourage the proper amount of carry on a short pitch shot.

To hit good pitch shots, you must zero in on a small target area—perhaps an imaginary circle of golf balls—on the green where the ball must land before rolling the rest of the way to the hole. Landing the ball short or long of the circle will throw off your distance control.

This is what's called doing the Circle Drill to perfection. The player picked a target inside the circle then hit it—dead center!

Practice Procedure: Designate a target on the green and, through trial and error, find the spot on the green where the ball must land in order to roll close to the hole time after time, using a variety of clubs. Mark this area by constructing a six-foot circle with string. In theory, if you choose the proper zone and land the ball in a six-foot circle, you'll always be inside three feet for your putt. Practice landing your short pitch shots inside the circle.

Repeat this drill using your seven-iron, nine-iron, pitching wedge, and wedge, and sixty-degree wedge, since the circle will move closer to the hole as you swing with a more lofted club. This drill provides vivid proof of this theory and will help your short game tremendously. For sure, you'll find your best chipping and pitching clubs and will be able to hit many more shots close to the cup.

LEFT-HAND-CONTROL DRILL

Problem: The player has no idea how to control the club with the left hand. Instead, he lets the right hand take control of the downswing.

Result: The player's direction is off. When playing short pitch shots, he either pushes or pulls the ball.

Goal: To find a way to make your left hand correctly play the lead role in controlling direction. When you pitch the ball, it's important that the left hand (the "direction hand") and the clubface arrive at impact lined up with each other in a square position. If the left hand turns left, you'll close the clubface and hit the ball left. If the left hand turns outward, the clubface will open and you'll hit the ball right of the target.

Practice Procedure: To enhance your feel for guiding the clubhead back to the ball at impact with your left hand, practice hitting short wedge shots with your left hand only. Grip more firmly if you have great difficulty returning the clubface squarely to the ball. Hit many short shots until you get the feel, then put the right hand on the club very lightly. This may give you added control and will allow you to sense left-hand control, too.

Hitting left-hand pitches will train your left hand to be the guide hand, particularly on the downswing where it really counts.

RIGHT-HAND PITCH DRILL

Problem: The player's pitch shots lack strength and feel.

Result: Approach shots often fall well short of the target.

Goal: To acquire shot-making feel and learn how to propel the ball to the hole.

To learn how to control distance, follow these steps for practicing the Right-Hand Pitch Drill.

Practice Procedure: Since your right hand is probably your strongest and also the most coordinated, it is the one you should use to set the club in the backswing and then feel the power required for delicate shots near the green. To help you learn how to control distance, practice hitting shots with your right hand only, each time varying the speed of the swing slightly. I've seen some of the worst pitch-shot players make a 180-degree turnaround using this drill.

After finishing the drill, put both hands on the club and hit shots to targets set out at different distances. The right-hand focus tends to encourage a true swinging action and a very natural-looking swing.

WALL DRILL

Problem: The player tends to get nervous on short pitch shots, stiffening up the wrists and making an overly wide, all-arms swing.

Result: He or she has great difficulty hitting soft, lofted pitch shots.

Goal: To learn how to swing the club back on a more upright plane—a prerequisite to hitting down sharply and lofting pitch shots into the air.

If you miss the wall on the backswing (left), you must also miss it on the way down (right) and learn to come into impact on a much steeper angle.

Practice Procedure: Place the club on the ground so that the clubhead is against the wall. You should then place your back foot near the grip end of the club. The distance between the wall and your back foot is the length of the club you are swinging.

Now swing back, trying to avoid hitting the wall with the club. You'll realize right away that in order to accomplish your goal of swinging on a more upright and narrow arc—and missing the wall—you'll have to hinge your wrists early in the takeaway.

DIVOT DRILL

Problem: The player fails to hit down sharply enough out of the rough. He or she tries to sweep the ball out.

Result: The player often hits a topped or thin shot.

Goal: To work on a drill that encourages you to learn and groove a steeper pitch swing, so you can recover nicely from heavy rough.

Practicing hitting shots out of divots will train you to steepen the plane of your swing and, in the process, become an expert recovery player from bad lies.

Practice Procedure: To learn to hit down on the ball, practice playing shots out of thin divot holes. Playing the ball back, with an open stance, will allow you to swing the club on a steeper plane. The steeper backswing plane is a technical "must" for promoting a sharp, descending hit at impact.

I learned this drill from former golf teacher and popular instructional book author John Andrisani. It is a wonderful quick fix for anyone whose swing arc is too shallow.

Divot Drill • 143

RIGHT–ARM
CROSS DRILL

This drill teaches you how to properly use your right arm and right shoulder during the swing.

KNEEL-DOWN-SWING DRILL

This drill teaches a level release.

RIGHT-ARM CROSS DRILL

This drill teaches you how to properly use your right arm and right shoulder during the swing.

RIGHT-ARM-ONLY ON-CENTER DRILL

This drill teaches you how to coordinate body and arm action during the swing.

SWING-UNDER-THE-SHAFT DRILL

This drill teaches you to feel a low takeaway action and also create a long flat spot through impact.

3

KNEEL-DOWN-
SWING DRILL

This drill teaches a level
release.

DRAW
DRILL #2

This drill will help you turn your slices into draws.

 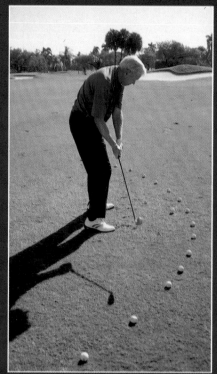

SHAFT-RESISTANCE DRILL

This drill will help you hit crisp, sharp chip and pitch shots.

SLAP-SHOT DRILL

This drill teaches you the important role the right hand, wrist, and arm play in allowing you to slap the sand with the bounce of a sand wedge and blast the ball out of a bunker.

TEE-CONTACT DRILL

This drill teaches you the hit-and-resist feel so vital to good short putting.

Chapter 7

CHIP LIKE A PRO

- *Proven drills for improving your chipping skills*

Getting up and down from around the green is an art, because being a good chipper means matching the right club and technique to the lie and distance of the shot.

When talking to high handicappers, many believe that chipping requires exceptional hand-eye coordination and natural touch. That's not really true. Anybody can develop good chipping skills, provided they practice. Besides, as I said in my original drills book, "Chipping incorporates correct swing path and correct clubface angle, position of the left wrist at impact and the relationship between the clubhead, hands, and body through the hitting area, the same factors you must deal with in the long game."

Chipping, like the full swing, requires wrist hinge, too, though to a smaller degree. A good chip stroke is not merely an extended arms-shoulders-controlled stroke, as many amateurs and so-called short-game experts believe. You need some wrist hinge to enhance your feel for the clubhead, to promote a slight descending hit, and to judge distance better. These vital elements of good chipping, along with several others, can be learned easily, provided you take the following course on chipping drills—where you learn everything from how to relieve tension in the stroke, to developing an on-path action, to the secrets for achieving solid and square impact—and study hard.

SPONGE-GRIP DRILL

Problem: The golfer holds the club too tightly with the left or "guide" hand, causing him or her to make a tense, overly stiff-armed, stiff-wristed chipping stroke.

Result: These faults lead to a lack of feel for the clubhead and poor distance control.

Goal: To learn to address the ball with light grip pressure and soft arms. Your wrists need to be "oily" to feel the weight of the clubhead in your hands. This overall softness through your arms, wrists, and hands will help you employ a smooth takeaway and allow the wrists to hinge naturally, which is essential for producing feel.

Practice Procedure: Squeeze a kitchen sponge very gently. Rehearse this degree of grip pressure in your mind. It may encourage you to increase the size of your grips. Large grips equal less wrists.

Next, take your favorite chipping club and grip it with the same amount of pressure you used when gripping the sponge. You should now be able to sense and feel the whole golf club. With light grip pressure, smoothly swing the arms and club back and forth with ease and tempo. Your shots will soon start to finish near the hole.

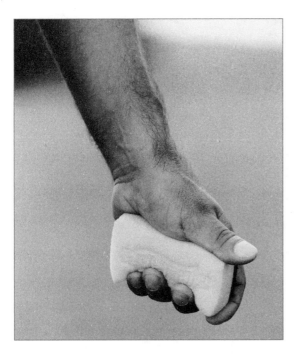

Squeeze a sponge very gently to help you learn to grip the club correctly on chip shots.

TENSION-RELIEVER DRILL

Problem: The player thinks so much about technique that he tenses up when chipping.

Result: The player ends up hitting skulls, chunks, and shanks.

Goal: To learn how to get out of the thinking mode so that your problem of standing over the ball too long and tensing up during the stroke will be ancient history.

Hitting rapid-fire chips and moving quickly from ball to ball will help you alleviate tension.

Practice Procedure: There's no way you can hit good chip shots when your muscles are tight. This drill, invented by Alabama-based teacher Conrad Rehling, will loosen you up. Anyone who has picked a driving range or hung out for long periods of time at a chipping range knows this drill.

Place several balls around the chipping green or in your backyard. Start the drill by walking up to the first ball, stepping into the shot then employing your chip stroke a split-second later. You must go directly from ball to ball in a brisk, machine-like fashion. Continue on, gradually sensing how well your arms, hands, hips, wrists, shoulders, and club move when you give yourself no time to think. Very often, I get great results using this drill as the student moves from shot to shot.

TROUGH DRILL *(Timeless Winner)*

Problem: The golfer swings the club well outside the target line on the backswing.

Result: He swings across the ball through impact, mishits the ball, and pulls the chip shot.

Goal: To learn to swing the club on the proper path and become a more consistent chipper.

The Trough Drill in pictures: Look and learn.

Practice Procedure: Take two clubs and form a narrow trough (as shown in the accompanying photograph) with a ball between it.

Using a seven-iron or your favorite chipping club, practice making strokes. The club should travel within the trough on the back- and through-swings. Once you learn to make solid contact and hit the ball on a consistent ball-flight line, change clubs.

When I was a young teacher, I was amazed at how difficult this drill was. However, after I got my students to make a short, sharp, on-line stroke, I always saw fantastic improvement. When I did the *Break 100* series on the Golf Channel, I taught this drill to my student David McClain. In less than five months, David dropped his handicap from thirty-six to fifteen. Much of the credit goes to this drill, which shows you the correct impact alignments and the basic move that all golfers need to learn for the full swing.

SHAFT-RESISTANCE DRILL

Problem: The player employs a level stroke, much like the one he or she uses to putt with.

Result: He or she has trouble consistently making solid contact with the ball and hitting the ball into the air.

Goal: To first understand the fundamentals of chipping. You must hit down on the ball to lift it in the air, even when using a sand wedge or sixty-degree wedge.

Practice Procedure: To fully understand the following drill, look closely at the photographs **(see color insert page 6).**

Take your normal chipping stance with your favorite club.

Next, have a friend hold a shaft about two feet above the ground in front of your left leg. Position the shaft so that the club will contact it if you go through too far. We ask our students to try and stop short of the shaft, and also to visualize the ball going under the shaft.

Then go ahead and swing, trying to hit the ball solidly without contacting the shaft. Don't worry. This drill will encourage you to take the club up on a slightly steeper plane and hit down more sharply. If you do all the right things, the ball will fly higher than you would ever expect and land softly on the green. Students are always amazed when they hit down on the ball and then see it fly over the shaft. I did several PGA workshops with legendary teacher Manuel de la Torre, and he demonstrated this tremendous drill, which is particularly good for beginners.

DISH-TOWEL DRILL

Problem: The player fails to hit easy chips near the hole.

Result: The player hits the ball well past or short of the hole.

Goal: To first understand what you need to do in order to succeed. When playing a lofted chip with a sand wedge, you must carry the ball almost all the way to the hole. The secret to hitting the ball within easy one-putt range is landing the ball on a preselected spot located just short of and in line with the hole.

Practice Procedure: To improve your touch, lay out a few small, white dish towels at different distances on your backyard lawn. Pace off the yardage to each. I suggest you lay these towels at five-yard increments from ten to thirty yards away. Now try to hit each towel.

Pitching to a dish-towel target will help improve your touch.

WATCHDOG DRILL

Problem: The player has poor hand-eye coordination.

Result: The player usually hits chips either well past the hole or short of it.

Goal: To improve your hand-eye coordination and distance control.

Watching the hole and chipping will teach you how to improve your distance control.

Practice Procedure: Take your normal chipping setup, placing the club-face of any chipping club squarely behind the ball and perpendicular to a hole some twenty-five feet away. Next, turn your head and look at the hole. Maintain that head position and make a smooth chip stroke. Hit about ten chips, each time watching how the ball reacts in the air and on the ground. Now, revert back to your normal address position, keeping your eyes on the ball. Hit the same number of shots with the same clubs. You'll see how much better your distance control is.

LEFT-WRIST PEN/PENCIL DRILL

Problem: The player's left arm and wrist collapse at impact.

Result: This fault causes poor distance and direction control.

Goal: To learn how to build a solid left-wrist and left-arm position that will promote solid chips.

Chipping with a pen or pencil under your watchband will train you to come into impact with a flat left wrist and hit solid, accurate shots.

Practice Procedure: This is an old faithful drill that's designed to help you lead the club into impact with a solid left arm and left wrist.

Stick a pen (or pencil) under your watchband, as shown in the accompanying photograph. This will automatically flatten the left (lead) wrist.

Now hit numerous short chip shots, making sure to brush the grass after hitting the ball with a slight downward strike. You'll quickly notice that the left wrist stays solid and firm through impact. It will probably be a totally new feel for some golfers. Stay with it, even if your initial results aren't as good as you'd like them to be.

Chapter 8

SAND SECRETS

- *Drills to help you hit good bunker shots*

As a teacher, I'm always looking for different ways to get my students to use the proper technique to recover from a bunker. Sometimes, one drill will work great for one student but not for another. That's why I like to have an arsenal of different drills and cures. I'm never sure which one will work best for each new golfer that visits a school for lessons or that I meet on the golf course.

The sand shot is actually easier to hit than most people think. It's the only shot in golf that requires that you don't hit the ball. Moreover, the sand wedge features a metal rudder called a "flange" or "bounce" that slides quite easily through the sand beneath the ball and splashes it out of the bunker.

I've been fortunate to have been around some truly imaginative and creative instructors and players, who have all helped me learn more about bunker-play techniques, including Claude Harmon, Sr., and Al Mengert, whose drills are included in this chapter, and Ken Venturi, who offered the Bunker-Play Tee Drill in the opening chapter.

In this chapter, I also include some other innovative drills that might better apply to your swing, most notably the Twenty-Five-Cent Bunker-Shot Drill from Glen Farnsworth, one of my top instructors at the Doral Golf Resort & Spa in Miami. I even offer you a drill that teaches you the technique needed to recover well from fairway bunkers.

I know that stepping into a bunker with confidence is one of the secrets to recovery. So experiment until you find the drill that helps you feel the most positive and employ a swing that lifts the ball out and over the lip and lands it next to—or into—the hole.

SLAP–SHOT DRILL

Problem: The player employs an overly short, stiff-wristed swing.

Result: He fails to hit a high, soft-landing shot.

Goal: To realize that bunker shots are very manageable once you know that half the battle is understanding that you must relax the arms at address, hinge the wrists freely early in the takeaway, and spank the sand behind the ball with the bounce of the club. The bounce, or flange, is the area of metal at the base of the club (below the leading edge) that allows the club to slide through the sand. It's like the wing of an airplane, and it prevents the clubhead from digging in.

Practice Procedure: This drill yields super-fast results, so look closely at the photographs **(see color insert page 7)**.

Set up open just slightly to the target, and with the club pointing at the hole, let go of the club with your left hand.

Next, make right-hand swings, like Claude Harmon taught me and many of his students at Winged Foot in New York, Thunderbird in California, and Seminole in Florida. All four of his sons, who are all tremendous instructors—Butch, Craig, Dick, and Bill—teach this drill. The more you practice this drill the more you will realize that the right hand, wrist, and arm control the width of the downswing and the hitting action. This is a very natural feeling once you get the hang of it. Just take your sand wedge and practice slapping an area of sand between two lines in the practice bunker and I guarantee you'll learn a lot about top bunker play.

DIFFICULT-LIES DRILL

Problem: The player hits good, basic sand shots, but is lost when facing a shot off a less than level lie.

Result: He hits bad shots and ruins his score.

Goal: To evolve into a versatile sand player.

Practice Procedure:

Throw several balls in a bunker and try to hit shots from the most difficult lies you can create. Repeat as necessary.

This drill will teach you, as it did Seve Ballesteros, to be so good out of bunkers that you will approach each shot on the course with the utmost confidence.

When practicing the Difficult-Lies Drill, your philosophy should be: The harder the lie, the bigger the challenge.

ERASE-THE-FOOTPRINT DRILL
(Timeless Winner)

Problem: On long bunker shots, the player digs much too deeply into the sand.

Result: The player leaves most shots short of the hole or inside the bunker.

Goal: To find out how to take less sand. The reason PGA Tour pros hit such good long bunker shots is that they swing on a shallow arc and take a shallow cut of sand. Conversely, amateurs pick the club up too quickly, then chop down and quit on the shot. The following drill, taught to me by my first professional instructor, Al Mengert, will train you to take a shallow cut of sand.

When practicing the Erase-the-Footprint Drill, place a ball in a footprint (left) and take a shallow cut of sand (center), so you erase or take out the footprint (right).

Practice Procedure: Make some light footprints in the sand. Swinging a sand wedge, try to brush through the length of the footprints, erasing each one. Make some new footprints, only this time put a ball in the center of them. Again, try to erase the footprint without ever thinking about the ball. It's great to see the golf ball come out every time. Use this drill and you'll get out of the sand like a pro every time.

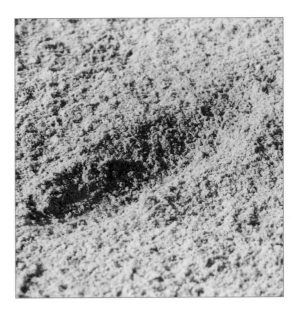

TWENTY-FIVE-CENT BUNKER-SHOT DRILL

Problem: The player turns his right hand and forearm over in a counterclockwise direction through impact, causing the face of the sand wedge to close.

Result: A low-flying shot that hits the wall of the bunker and rolls back down into it.

Goal: To learn how to maintain an open clubface position in the hitting area and blast the ball up over the lip.

Start the Twenty-Five-Cent Bunker-Shot Drill by putting sand and a quarter on the face of your sand wedge (left). Swing from address directly into the follow-through, making sure to keep the sand and quarter on the clubface (center). Make an actual swing, matching the perfect follow-through position you rehearsed, then watch your ball carry the lip and head toward the target (right).

Practice Procedure: Here's a drill from one of my teachers, Glen Farnsworth.

Open the face of a sand wedge, then put a little sand and a quarter on it. Next, take your normal stance and posture.

Then, without taking a backswing, go directly to the halfway-through position by releasing the triangle formed by your arms and shoulders, plus your right knee and right hip. If the quarter stays in place, you are making great progress.

Now, complete the drill by actually hitting bunker shots. Employ a three-quarter-length backswing, then swing down and skim the sand with the bounce of the club, returning to the same, previous finish position.

FRONT-LINE DRILL

Problem: The player swings on too flat of a plane when hitting fairway-bunker shots, either hitting behind the ball or not making clean contact.

Result: The ball flies so low that it hits the bunker's lip and falls back down into the sand, or the player constantly chunks fairway bunker shots.

Goal: To learn how to employ a specialized swing that makes for solid contact with the ball and lifts it well over the lip.

Concentrating on trying to hit the ball, rather than the line in the sand, will help promote a descending blow and clean contact.

Practice Procedure: This drill will teach how to win the battle with a fairway bunker and make you so confident that you'll welcome the challenge of playing this type of shot.

Draw a straight line perpendicular to the target line in the sand. Set a ball down just ahead of the line, so that it is positioned practically opposite the midpoint in your stance.

Swing back and then through, making sure to contact the ball first. You will see that the position of the ball promotes a hands-ahead setup position, a more upright swing, and a descending blow. It feels good to hit the ball cleanly, doesn't it? Now try to hit a whole line of balls solidly. If you hit an extra-low shot or hit behind the line, start over, concentrating on keeping your body very steady and accelerating the arms and club through the impact zone.

Chapter 9
CURING PUTTING WOES

- *Drills to help you cure putting problems*

Every professional and amateur needs good putting drills. I say this because just going to a putting green with three balls and no plan is extremely boring, not to mention unproductive.

Golf is played in the air except on the greens, where it is completely a ground game. Included in this chapter are numerous unique drills that can help you with every aspect of the "other game." The better your stroke and the better you roll the ball, the more putts you will sink. However, there is more to good putting than just a pure roll. You must also be a good green-reader to allow for the right amount of break. Further, you must be able to control the speed of the putt so that you don't hit the ball through the break or leave the ball on the low side of the hole.

Don't worry. These drills cover much of what you'll need to know about putting. Bring one or more of these drills with you the next time you schedule some putting practice, and I know the results will be good.

ONE-BALL PRACTICE DRILL

Problem: The player loses his or her concentration when putting. Or, he or she always practices with multiple balls yet fails to improve.

Result: Poor putting scores on the golf course, particularly in tournaments.

Goal: To find a way to enhance your mental focus and simulate real golf situations.

Practicing with one ball will ultimately make you concentrate harder on the course.

Practice Procedure: Practice with just one ball instead of throwing a few balls down on the green and putting without focus, as many poor putters typically do. Use your on-course putting routine and concentrate on every stroke. Following this one-ball practice procedure will intensify your concentration, as sports coach and friend Dr. Fran Pirozzolo advocates. More important, you'll carry this intense mind-set to the course and see quick improvement in your putting scores. Use your on-course routine and try to create "game conditions." Make your practice much like the real thing.

BALL-DROP DRILL

Problem: The player's head is not positioned on or close to the target line.

Result: The player consistently pulls or pushes short putts.

Goal: To learn to position your eyes directly over the ball or over a spot on the target line behind the ball. Either of these positions will encourage a straight-back, straight-through putting stroke.

The Ball-Drop Drill will help you position your head correctly at address.

Practice Procedure: Assume your normal putting stance, with the ball played just inside your left heel.

Hold a ball next to the bridge of your nose then drop it. If the ball lands well inside or outside the target line, change your head position. I particularly do not like the eyes outside the line.

Repeat this exercise until the ball consistently drops on the one you addressed or on the target line itself, behind the ball.

WHISTLE-WHILE-YOU-PUTT DRILL

Problem: The player has trouble making a rhythmic stroke because he or she thinks too much.

Result: Poor distance control.

Goal: To find a way to putt more by feel.

Whistling while you practice putting will help you think less about technique and concentrate more on feeling the proper rhythmic action.

Practice Procedure: When practicing putting on your own, do what former Masters and U.S. Open winner Fuzzy Zoeller does in practice, and in play. Try whistling as you address the ball and stroke it. You can whistle very quietly. Doing this will take your mind off technique and allow you to accomplish your goal.

RUNNING–START DRILL

Problem: The player picks the putter up in the takeaway.

Result: This fault promotes mishits and sometimes a faulty chop action at impact, rather than a smooth, level stroke.

Goal: To learn how to keep the putter low to the ground going back, so that it's delivered into the ball level. A level stroke that allows you to strike the equator of the ball will promote a pure roll of the ball.

Starting with the putterhead about four inches behind the ball will help you groove a flowing, level takeaway action.

Practice Procedure: This is a drill I have used for a variety of problems with the takeaway. When practicing putts, place the putterhead about four inches behind the ball, instead of directly behind it to promote a low takeaway. You may also hold the putterhead slightly off the ground to alleviate tension and promote a big-muscle-controlled stroke.

IMPROVE-YOUR-"READING"-SKILLS DRILL

Problem: The player fails to read greens at all or continually misreads putts.

Result: He tends to miss breaking putts, even short ones.

Goal: To increase your green-reading skills so that you hole a higher percentage of curving putts.

When practicing putting, get accustomed to reading the breaks from different angles.

Practice Procedure: Find a large practice putting green. Hit putts from different distances and with different curves, being sure to read the putt from behind the ball, behind the hole, and from each side. Discover where you best see the true break. Take this pre-swing routine to the course, making sure not to take too much time between "reads." Remember, green-reading is probably the most underrated aspect of good putting. If you cannot determine the correct line you'll have to mis-stroke the putt to make it. Carl Welty, who I regard as one of the finest putting teachers in the world, has proved to me over and over that golfers often change their strokes on opposite breaking putts without realizing it. That is usually because they under-read the break and have to push or pull the putter to get the ball on or near the line.

BELLY-PUTTER DRILL

Problem: The player fails to swing the putter along a naturally arcing path, with the putter opening going back and closing going through.

Result: The player's distance and direction control is inconsistent.

Goal: To learn to groove a pure, pendulum putting stroke.

The Belly-Putter Drill: Address (left), backswing (center), and downswing (right).

Practice Procedure: Practice with a forty-three- to forty-six-inch-long belly-putter to improve your stroke.

Most of us have heard of a pendulum stroke but often do not truly understand what it is and how it applies to putting. The idea behind it is this: The pendulum of a clock swings from a fixed and anchored spot. This fixed position remains constant, causing the pendulum to swing and arc naturally. The belly-putter achieves this motion in a putting stroke.

First, begin with practice strokes, and then hit putts on the putting green. You will see that the putter arcs slightly to the inside and then back to the inside as the putter-face releases. The shorter the putt the less this will happen. You will feel a perfect pendulum stroke.

Practicing with the belly-putter will likely help your conventional stroke, and you may even find yourself putting a belly-putter into your bag sometime soon. Believe it or not, legendary player and teacher Paul Runyan advocated this style of putting more than forty years ago.

RIGHT-HAND-AND-ARM PUTTING DRILL

Problem: The player's stroke is too mechanical and tense.

Result: The fault causes him or her to leave the ball short of the hole.

Goal: To learn a natural putting stroke that rolls the ball purely and promotes good distance control.

Swinging the putter back with your right hand only (left) then through the ball (right) will help you develop a more consistent stroke.

Practice Procedure: There are two people who come to my mind when I recommend this right-hand-and-arm putting drill: teacher Jack Burke, Jr., who greatly influenced the putting strokes of Ben Crenshaw and Jack Nicklaus, and my friend Bob Ford, the head professional at two of the top ten golf courses in America, Oakmont and Seminole. Both use this as a staple drill.

Take a page out of the lesson books of these two great teachers and practice putting with just your dominant hand and arm. As they explain to their students, and I to mine, this drill allows you to feel how the right side (for right-hand players) controls the speed of the putter and the act of propelling the ball smoothly across the green to the hole.

Once you get a feel for the right-side hit, take a full grip to appreciate how the left hand and arm play the lead role in the stroke when it comes to direction—or just hit putts left-handed next!

NARROW-OPENING PUTTING DRILL

Problem: The player tends to hit some putts off the toe of the putter and others off its heel. On-center hits are rare.

Result: Poor distance and direction control.

Goal: To learn to repeat a solid stroke and consistently hit the ball with the sweet spot of the putter.

Practice Procedure: I learned the following drill from Bill Davis, the head golf professional at Jupiter Hills Golf Club in Tequesta, Florida.

Place two golf balls parallel to the target line with just enough room between them for your putter to swing freely through. Practice without a ball for several minutes to establish whether you can move the putter through the opening repeatedly. If you strike the outside ball, your putter is looping out in some fashion. This fault will cause a heel-hit. If you hit the inside ball, you'll know that you're pulling the putter inward, causing toe-hits. To correct either mistake, adjust your stance, head position, grip pressure, or shoulder alignment.

Next, begin to hit putts at the hole, first from a short distance then from twenty feet. Does your stroke change? If yes, determine why and make adjustments. You can either tighten the gap between the balls or widen it as you first begin the improvement process.

Hitting putts through
a narrow opening of
balls will train you to
employ a square and
solid on-path stroke.

HORIZONTAL-SHAFT DRILL

Problem: The player's speed control is inconsistent.

Result: He or she leaves putts in the ten- to fifteen-foot range short of the hole.

Goal: To improve the player's speed control so that all putts have a chance of going into the cup.

Practice Procedure: This is one of my favorite drills, which I also learned from golf pro and renowned short-game instructor Bill Davis.

Depending on the length of the putt, the slope of the green, and the general conditions of grain, place a clubshaft at various distances behind the cup. You can do this on the practice putting green or when you play alone on the course.

For a flat, ten-foot putt, I generally place the shaft eight inches behind the hole. I then ask the student to strike numerous putts, say fifty. For each putt that goes in the hole, or hits the shaft on the ground, the player gets one point. With that in mind, you would think winning is automatic. The kicker is, for any putt left short, you lose fifty points.

This really gets you to focus on speed control. Being short is not an option. By the way, if you hit a putt so hard that it jumps the shaft on the ground, you lose ten points. Therefore, you cannot blindly smash putts, either.

Practicing the
Horizontal-Shaft Drill
will enhance your
speed control on
putts.

HIGH-SIDE DRILL

Problem: The player fails to hit the ball on the high side of the hole on sharply breaking putts.

Result: He or she hits weakly breaking putts that have no chance of going in the hole.

Goal: To learn how to better control the speed of the putt and confidently hit the ball on the high side of the hole, so that it has a chance of dropping into the cup.

Practice Procedure: Take several balls to the practice green and, if possible, make this a betting game with a friend. Start with a ten-foot breaking putt.

Lay out a row of balls, leading to the hole, as illustrated. Place a shaft on the ground to serve as a guide for hitting the ball on the high side of the hole. You want to direct the ball between the row of balls and the clubshaft, to ensure a high-side putt. Place a head cover just short of the hole and on the low side.

For every putt you make you win two dollars. For every putt you miss, but hit on the high side, you win one dollar. So it would seem very easy to win at least forty dollars. All you have to do is miss every putt on the high side and hit it hard enough to go past the hole. That should be easy enough, right? The problem is, if you miss the putt low and hit the headcover, you lose forty dollars. It doesn't take long doing this drill to learn to get your putts on the high side and past the hole.

Practicing in this putting workstation will train you to hit breaking putts on the high side of the hole.

TEE-CONTACT DRILL

Problem: On short putts, the player has trouble coming into impact with the putter face at a right angle to the hole. Furthermore, he has no concept of the vital hit-and-resist feel common to all great short-distance putters.

Result: The player hits off-line putts more often than not.

Goal: To learn a pro-type stroke that will ensure dead-square contact and, for that reason, make the player more confident over pressure putts.

Practice Procedure: This putting drill (**see color insert page 8**) is a favorite among our school students.

Place two tees firmly into the putting surface, leaving just enough width for a ball to go through. Place a ball between the tees. Strike the ball. Your putter will stop against the tees. Make certain that both ends of the putter-head contact the tees at the same time, since this signals dead-square contact. Again, the head of the putter will stop as it meets the tees. Hold this stop position for two seconds, or until you get physically acquainted with the all-important hit-and-resist feel.

Chapter 10
TROUBLE-SHOOTER DRILLS

- *Drills designed to help you cure your shot-making ailments—everything from a slice, to a duck hook, to a fat shot, to a shank*

Every golfer hits occasional bad shots due to a faulty setup or swing.

In this chapter, I cover every ugly shot—from the big slice to the shank—and offer at least one remedy and sometimes multiple cures for each.

I think you'll find this chapter very educational and helpful. You'll learn that there are different types of left-to-right shots, the most dramatic being the slice, and various forms of right-to-left shots, with the duck hook being the most outrageous. You'll learn, too, how the cure must be very specific. For that reason, before picking a drill to practice, analyze your ball flight carefully to see exactly what shot-making "ailment" you're suffering from. Alternatively, have a friend watch you hit balls, and listen to what he or she observes.

Something else that's good about this chapter is that it teaches you the cause and effect of certain body and club movements. The more you learn, the better able you'll be to pinpoint a problem and solve it on the course before a good round gets away from you.

ANTI-SLICE DRILL #1 *(Timeless Winner)*

Problem: The player swings the club on a faulty swing path on the backswing and over-rotates the left side on the downswing.

Result: The player hits a slice.

Goal: To learn the proper "job description" of the left side during the downswing and ingrain the physical movements necessary for producing an inside-square-inside swing path.

Hitting balls from an angled setup position (left) will help you learn to approach the ball from the inside (right).

Practice Procedure: Set up to a teed up ball with a seven-iron, setting the clubface down perpendicular, or square, to the target. Now turn your body forty-five degrees to the right (away from the target), dropping your right foot back but continuing to aim the clubface at your initial target. You will feel super-closed and the clubface will look very closed, but that's okay—this is exactly what I want.

Hit balls from this unorthodox setup position, each time feeling the club approach the ball from inside the line of play. You almost cannot possibly hit from the outside, and that's why the drill is so effective. Hitting against a firm left leg, together with rotating the arms and hands, is automatic, and you cannot slice! It's a guaranteed hook.

Once you get accustomed to hitting hook shots doing this drill, you're ready to take your normal square setup with this new swing image, and bring your slice-proof swing to the golf course. Just remember the swing path you used to hit these draws and hook. You must repeat that same "attack track" from the squared-off stance. Enjoy your new power!

ANTI-SLICE DRILL #2

Problem: The player fails to release the club properly on the downswing.

Result: The player slices the ball.

Goal: To discover a drill especially designed to teach the proper release action of the hands, arms, and club, and to cure a dramatic left-to-right slice shot.

Anti-Slice Drill #2 in pictures:
Look and learn.

Practice Procedure: Select a seven-iron. Grip the club extra lightly, but set it down with the toe of the clubhead perpendicular to the ground. From here, simply swing the club halfway back and halfway through. As you swing through, let the toe of the club hit the ground first. Feel the head rotate over as your forearms rotate through impact.

Implement this feel into your swing and your slice will disappear, as students of one my teachers, Glen Farnsworth, discover practically on a daily basis.

ANTI-PUSH CONNECTION DRILL

(Timeless Winner)

Problem: The player's left arm strays too far from the body—it disconnects on the forward swing. The clubface is delivered into an open, rather than square, impact position.

Result: A classic block-shot hit right of the target.

Goal: To keep the left arm connected to the body so that you ensure a square clubface position at impact and hit powerfully accurate shots.

Place a glove under your upper left arm (left), then swing back (center) and through (right), keeping the glove trapped.

Practice Procedure: Place a glove or a small towel under the upper portion of your left arm, then take your address position. Swing back and through, keeping your left arm snugly against your chest so that the glove stays in a trapped position.

When working on this drill—one that teacher Jimmy Ballard taught former PGA champion Hal Sutton and me many years ago—you'll find it necessary to allow your left arm to fold at the elbow on the follow-through. It may exaggerate the release action, but it's evidence that you've used your arms and hands with your body motion to square the clubface.

I've used this drill with PGA Tour professionals Len Mattiace, Tom Kite, and Cristie Kerr, to name just a few, and it really works.

ANTI-WEAK-FADE DRILL

Problem: The golfer exaggerates the leg action on the downswing.

Result: This fault causes him or her to get ahead of the ball and ultimately hit a weak fade.

Goal: To stabilize the left side through the impact zone and keep the golfer from getting ahead of the shot.

This drill teaches you how to stabilize the left side through impact.

Practice Procedure: I have had a lot of success with this particular drill, using it to help both amateurs and tour pros.

Hit practice shots with your left heel off the ground. Better yet, place a golf ball (or the grip end of a golf club) under your left heel. Immediately, you should feel the left side brace up through impact. You will not be able to spin out or go ahead of the shot.

My first teacher, Al Mengert, taught me this drill when I was just a teenager, and he first had me tee up each ball until I learned to develop feel and lower-body stability. This is good advice for you. Al was a big believer in lower-body resistance, and this drill certainly gives you that feel. By the way, Al worked for two of golf's greatest teachers: Claude Harmon, at Winged Foot in Mamaroneck, New York, and Tommy Armour, at the Boca Raton Resort and Club in Boca Raton, Florida.

ANTI-BIG-BLOCK DRILL

Problem: The player's head drifts forward and the lower body slides on the downswing.

Result: These faults cause the golfer to become trapped when swinging down and hit a big block right of the target.

Goal: To learn to stay behind the ball through impact, so you give yourself time to square up the clubface.

Keep your eyes on the red stripe on the ball to help groove a stay-behind-the-ball through-swing movement.

Practice Procedure: Tee up a golf ball with a red range-stripe painted on its back equator. At address, you should be able to clearly see the marking on the ball. If not, move the ball forward in your stance.

Now, swing a seven-iron, concentrating on seeing "red" when you swing back and then through. Go ahead and make an aggressive swing, focusing each time on the mark.

On the golf course, you can do the same thing on every tee shot. Simply concentrate on the ball's logo on the back part of the ball and hit it right in the "button." The result: a powerful, accurate tee shot.

ANTI-WAYWARD-CUT CLOCK DRILL

Problem: The player swings on an exaggerated outside-in path.

Result: The golfer frequently hits wayward cut shots.

Goal: To understand the arcing action of the swing.

Practice swinging down from seven o'clock to one o'clock and you'll become a more powerfully accurate ball-striker.

Practice Procedure: Here is the oldest drill (and visual image) that I use at my schools. We have used it in every opening presentation since 1986. I've noticed that quite a few professionals have copied how we use the numbers and how we color-code the clock placed on the ground. I actually got the idea for the clock concept from teacher Craig Harmon at a seminar we did together for the PGA of America. Craig said to visualize your swing going from seven to one on a clock laid down flat on the ground. Craig drew a line on the ground indicating the path line.

Later I saw Craig Shankland, another PGA member, use a coded board to show the correct and incorrect paths. So, using both, I actually began to use golf balls to illustrate the hours on a clock, with the target line extending from six to twelve o'clock. It became the most important aspect of every golf school opening beginning back in the 1980s.

The idea is to understand and then actually execute a swing that approaches the ball from seven o'clock toward one o'clock. To hit the ball straight over twelve o'clock and down the target line, you must actually hit from the inside. This, I think, just might be the single most difficult concept for most golfers to comprehend, so keep practicing until your club can tell time.

ANTI-DUCK-HOOK FORTY-FIVE-DEGREE DRILL

Problem: The player swings on an exaggerated inside-out path. Furthermore, his or her upper body hangs back through impact.

Result: These two faults cause him to flip the clubface closed and hit a duck hook.

Goal: To correct a faulty inside-out path and learn to work the upper body properly, so that you move fluidly into impact with a square clubface and cure your duck-hook problem.

This drill is weird looking, but it will cure a duck-hook problem.

Practice Procedure: Grip a seven-iron. Set up with your back foot turned out about forty-five degrees and the ball positioned well forward.

Now, make relatively easy golf swings, using your shoulders and upper body to do all of the work. This procedure will get you out of the habit of firing the legs too early, causing the upper body to hang back.

As you increase speed and improve your ball flight, go to a longer iron, such as a five-iron. Now actually hit fades with the same setup. Make sure the ball starts left and fades back to the target. I've used this drill with many low handicappers, club professionals, and tour pros with excellent results. It is definitely a more advanced player's drill, but it can work wonders for any level of player. That, I guarantee.

ANTI-DUCK-HOOK BOX DRILL

Problem: The player follows a friend's advice to swing out at the ball.

Result: He finds he cannot stop hooking the ball far to the left of the target.

Goal: To learn to swing the club on the proper inside-square-inside path and hit accurate shots.

Practicing with a shoe box near the ball will discourage you from swinging out at the ball.

Practice Procedure: Place a shoe box just outside of the golf ball that's teed up slightly.

Swing. If your swing is inside-out at all, you'll nick the shoe box after impact, so you get instant feedback. You quickly learn that the golf club must swing back to the left after impact, something that many golfers fail to comprehend.

My good friend Tom Kite, the 1992 U.S. Open champion, uses this drill all the time, only he uses a two-by-four instead of a shoebox. In the many hours we have spent together working on his full swing, this is the one drill that has never changed. Tom always goes back to the board because he never wants the golf club swinging out to the right after impact. I cannot tell you how many thousands of shots I have seen Tom hit using the board.

ANTI-SWEEP-HOOK SWING-LEFT DRILL

Problem: The golfer tends to swing down underneath the plane.

Result: He or she hits a sweeping hook.

Goal: To swing down on the correct plane and hit the ball accurately.

Matching up two shafts at address (left) and in the through-swing (right) will help you get rid of a sweep-hook problem.

Practice Procedure: Place a golf shaft at an angle in front of your body, as shown. When you set up, the angle of the clubshafts—the shaft in the ground and the one in the club you're holding—should match up.

Swing back.

Swing through, trying again to match up the two shafts. At first, you will feel as though the club is swinging immediately left after impact. You will also feel a very high right side. This is okay. Also, make sure to keep your upper-left arm (lead arm) connected to the left side of your body. Additionally, make certain to allow your left elbow to fold down and your right arm to straighten as you rotate through into a three-quarter finish. Hold that finish.

Practice this drill an hour a day for a week. Soon, you'll be swinging on-plane and hitting straight bullet shots.

ANTI-PULL RELEASE DRILL

Problem: The player swings the club into a poor position at the top of the swing.

Result: He or she ends up pulling the club through impact and blocking shots left and right.

Goal: To set the club in a square position at the top of the swing and deliver it squarely to the ball at impact. A good swing is on-plane with the arms swinging on a slightly more upright arc than the shoulders. However, regardless of the angle of the plane, there should be a certain amount of rotation of the left arm during the backswing. If your swing lacks this left-arm rotation, the wrist may close or open as it moves along its arc. To promote the correct square clubface position, practice the following drill.

Mimic my baseball-type swing in practice and you won't pull the ball in play.

Practice Procedure: Stand up straight and hold the club at waist height. Next, swing the club around you like a baseball bat. Notice how the left forearm gradually rotates clockwise. This is the action you should strive for.

Next, begin to lower the club to the ball as you tilt toward the ball.

As you swing back, feel as if the club is gradually opening. The club-face is actually staying square to the swing's arc, and that is precisely the action you want to encourage.

ANTI-HEEL-SHOT WHIFF DRILL

Problem: The player comes into impact with either the heel or neck of the club striking the ball.

Result: A shank or some sort of bad shot hit off the heel of the golf club.

Goal: To learn to return the club to a square impact position and hit more on-target shots.

Address the outside ball then hit the inside ball to cure a heel-hit problem.

Practice Procedure: Place two golf balls down on the ground, side by side, approximately three inches apart. Set up to the ball farthest from you.

Swing back and then down trying to strike the inside ball while missing or "whiffing" the ball you originally addressed. If you fail, try again. If you succeed, figure out how you did it by getting in tune with the movements of the club and your body. Some golfers will feel an inside loop, while others will feel the hands in closer to the body at impact. You may feel something entirely different, and that's okay. I just want you to realize and then feel that you have been swinging the heel of the club out to strike the ball. This drill will likely get you back to making on-center contact. What a relief it will be to feel the solid strike of a correct swing.

ANTI-TOE-HIT WHIFF DRILL

Problem: The player swings the club back into the ball on an exaggerated outside-in path with poor extension.

Result: He or she comes into impact with the toe of the club leading the way, rather than its center or sweet spot.

Goal: To hit accurate shots by learning how to return the club squarely to the ball.

Address the inside ball then hit the outside ball to cure a toe-hit problem.

Practice Procedure: Line up two balls approximately four inches apart. Set up to the ball nearest you.

Swing back and then through, trying to strike the outside ball while missing or "whiffing" the inside ball. To accomplish this goal, you will need an entirely different feel and new swing thought. Previously, you had been sucking the arms and club inward toward your body. Now you must do the opposite—feel a huge expansion of the hands and arms out and through impact.

Try easy swings at first, then increase your speed as you feel yourself extending your arms and making square clubface-to-ball contact.

ANTI-POWER-LOSS IMPACT DRILL

Problem: When driving, the player has poor impact alignments. This is bad, because square contact is as important to hitting the ball powerfully as generating high clubhead speed is.

Result: The player loses power.

Goal: To promote swing power and distance by learning to vastly improve impact alignments.

Improve your impact alignments by swinging through the ball into an impact bag.

Practice Procedure: Set up to a ball at the base of an impact bag, which can be purchased at your local golf shop or sporting goods store. At first, practice striking the impact bag at very low speed. Once you can achieve excellent impact alignments, increase your speed, but never hit the impact bag very hard because it can bend your club.

Swing a five-iron, trying to hit the ball but also being aware of the impact bag just ahead of it. Strive for those solid impact alignments shown in the photo. Once you feel the ball is simply getting in the way, remove the impact bag and test yourself. If you continue hitting good shots, switch to the driver. If your swing and ball-striking go bad, just use the impact bag until you get your alignments right.

I first used this drill with great success on Rick Hartmann, a former European tour player who taught at my schools before moving on to become the Director of Golf at Atlantic, a prestigious club on Long Island.

ANTI-FLAT-SWING POWER-LOSS DRILL

Problem: The player's backswing path is so flat that he fails to correctly return the clubface squarely to the ball at impact.

Result: Weak shots.

Goal: To learn how to swing the club on a more upright plane and achieve power-generating clubface-to-ball contact.

Practicing with this umbrella will help you un-groove a flat swing.

Practice Procedure: Set up to a ball with a five-iron. Next, have a friend place an umbrella approximately two feet behind your right heel.

Swing back. If the club contacts the umbrella, your swing is too flat. Make numerous practice swings until you are certain you will miss the umbrella—on the way up and on the way down. Before you hit the ball, move the umbrella back six to ten inches. You must put the umbrella in a position where you will not hit it on the downswing. When hitting, use the umbrella just as a reminder. Move it back into position for practice swings only.

ANTI-POWER-LOSS HEAD-COVER DRILL

Problem: The player keeps the right elbow too close to the body, causing his or her swing to lose width and the muscles to tense up.

Result: The player loses distance.

Goal: To learn to free up the right elbow so that power is created and preserved on the backswing.

Practice Procedure: Place a head cover under your right armpit. This effectively locks in the upper-right arm.

Take your backswing, letting the right elbow move away from your body without "flying." If you make the right moves, the head cover will fall out. If you tense up, the head cover will stay in place.

I've watched Masters and PGA champion Vijay Singh do many drills on the range, including this one to increase his backswing width. If you need to free up your arm swing and create more power, take a cure from this great player.

The head cover should be snugly under your left arm at address, then fall out on the backswing.

ANTI-FAT-SHOT DRILL

Problem: The player keeps his head down too long in an attempt to keep his or her eyes on the ball.

Result: The player gets stuck in the impact zone, jamming the head of an iron into the ground behind the ball and taking a fat divot.

Goal: To learn to make solid contact with the ball before cutting a thin divot out of the fairway grass.

"Peeking" before impact just may cure your fat-shot problem.

Practice Procedure: Take a page out of the lesson books of top pros Annika Sorenstam, Justin Leonard, David Duval, and Jim Furyk. An interesting move that all of them make—and one reason that they're such good ball-strikers (not one of them takes deep divots)—is that they actually take their eyes off the ball *before* impact. Each player lets the head release extra early, with the eyes looking down the target line. If you tend to lock in and stay back and down too long, this drill is for you. I know it helped a young Brad Faxon become a better player when I began working with him in 1990.

Don't get stuck looking at a vacant spot on the ground at the end of what is almost certainly very inhibiting swing. In truth, you don't necessarily need to see the ball. If you don't believe me, ask blind golfer Pat Browne, who regularly breaks eighty.

ANTI-WEDGE-CHUNK-SHOT SHALLOW-WEDGE DRILL

Problem: The player's backswing is too steep.

Result: This fault causes him or her to come into impact from too steep an angle and chunk wedge shots—hit the ground behind the ball and take out a deep divot.

Goal: To shallow-out the plane of the swing so it's ideal for hitting crisp, twenty- to fifty-yard pitch shots.

Practice Procedure: Here's a drill that PGA Tour professional Len Mattiace invented as we worked on shallowing-out his pitching game.

Grip any wedge. Close your foot-line, but keep your shoulders open.

Make a normal backswing, following your shoulder-line.

On the way down, return the club along a path close to your foot-line. This will ensure a shallow attack-track. As you start the forward swing, a good mental image is to think of the arms falling or the clubhead dropping downward. The closed stance helps tremendously. So much so that Lenny uses it when playing in tournaments.

Hitting balls from this setup position—closed feet, open shoulders—may help you stop chunking wedge shots.

ANTI-SHANK DRILL #1

Problem: The player swings the club on such an exaggerated out-to-in path that the neck or shank of the club contacts the ball.

Result: A shank shot that darts dead right.

Goal: To learn to swing on the correct path so square contact is made and the ball flies directly at the target.

Anti-Shank Drill #1: Address (left), backswing (center), downswing (right).

Practice Procedure: When reading about this drill, look closely at the accompanying photograph, so you can set your props correctly in place.

Place four tees around your golf ball. Tee your ball in the same spot, shot after shot. Place three tees four inches ahead of this ball, in line with it. Tee number two is directly on your target line and the other two tees (numbers one and three) are on each side. Place these tees two inches apart. Place tee number four directly on-line with the outside tee and about four inches behind the ball. This will give you eight inches of room between the two outside tees.

Once you set up, place the clubhead behind the ball. You will notice just enough clearance to miss the single tee on your takeaway. Your goal is to hit the outside tee (number three) as you go through the shot, while missing the back tee. This will give you an inside attack. At first, you might often hit the back tee. That's okay—just keep replacing it. You might also continue to miss the outside forward tee (number three). This is okay, too. If you do hit this tee while missing number four, you'll be swinging from inside-out, or opposite to the way you swung before beginning this drill. This drill accentuates the in-to-out swing action, so you'll eventually want to miss tee number four and take out tee number two.

ANTI-SHANK DRILL #2

Problem: The player's shaft position is "laid off," or dramatically pointing left of the target at the top.

Result: The player swings down so far from the inside that he or she hits the ball with the club's neck or shank.

Goal: To develop a more upright swing and stop hitting shank shots.

The Anti-Shank Drill #2: From start to finish.

Practice Procedure: I spent many hours with Gardner Dickinson, the late, great player and teacher, and on one occasion he showed me this drill for curing a shank.

Take your pitching wedge and assume a balanced setup. Stick a tee in the vent hole of the club's grip. Now grip down about three inches.

Swing the club back to the three-quarter position, making certain that the tee points toward the ground, almost vertically. Gardner would say to a student: "Stand the club up."

Next, swing the club down like a ceiling fan turned on its side. This will take away the rolling of the hands in the backswing and will quickly give you the feeling of a less rounded swing. A more up-and-down, back-and-through swing virtually guarantees that you will never hit a shank.

Chapter 11
MIND GAMES

- *Mental drills to help you raise the level of your total tee-to-green game*

I've always been a big believer in teaching the whole game of golf. All of my instructors at every facility are thoroughly trained in the "Twenty-Five Percent Theory." This is a concept I've spoken about since 1982 and the centerpiece of my teaching system.

The Twenty-Five Percent Theory divides golf into four equal areas: the long game, the short game, the management game, and the mental game. Naturally, the drills in this book focus mostly on the long and short game, but also include stretching and strengthening drills (Chapter Two), which are part of the management area.

It might seem odd to also add a section devoted to the mental game. It might even be argued that what follows are mental concepts rather than mental drills. Be that as it may, anyone who has ever played golf knows that a huge part of the game is played between the ears. Therefore, I included this chapter in the hope that some of these mental drills will make a significant difference in how you play golf.

Professional golfers might say that golf is 90 percent mental. Of course, that's because they are already so good at the other aspects of golf. However, it is an undeniable fact that golf is more of a mental game than any other sport.

Study these mental drills and I'm sure a few of them will improve your state of mind on the golf course. They'll also allow you to be more imaginative, so that you'll see the shot come to life in your mind before swinging—"go to the movies" as Jack Nicklaus says. This cinematic pre-swing procedure, my fellow golfers, is, in fact, one of the paramount secrets to employing a good golf swing and hitting good golf shots.

PACIFIC OCEAN DRILL

Problem: The golfer concentrates on trouble spots bordering the fairway, namely deep rough and water, rather than focusing on a landing area in the "short grass."

Result: This common fault causes the player to steer the club in the opposite direction of the trouble and hit an off-line shot, while on other occasions the player will hit the ball exactly where he feared hitting it. For example, the golfer who fears hitting a ball down the left side into the water will tend to steer the club well out to the right and block the ball into an equally penal hazard.

Goal: To use an image that frees you up mentally and physically, so that you make a flowing, accelerated swinging action.

Pretending you're hitting into a big body of water will help you make an uninhibited swing.

Practice Procedure: When setting up to hit drives on the practice range, imagine that you are hitting into a large body of water. This is a tip I got many years ago from two-time major championship winner Jackie Burke. The water is such a big target that you just let the club rip like John Daly. Take this same image with you to the course.

Jack Burke, Jr. actually had me take balls down to Galveston, Texas and hit them from the beach into the Gulf of Mexico. When I came back to Houston and reported that I hit all of these shots very well, Burke said, "That's it, McLean, you dumb son of a gun . . . you have to let go and have some abandonment in your swing. You can't steer it." I tell people to aim at the Pacific Ocean because it's an even bigger target. Heck, there is no way to miss, so let go.

RING-OF-FIRE DRILL

Problem: The player experiences first-tee jitters and can't take his or her mind off the trees, rough, and water bordering the fairway.

Result: The player makes a nervous swing and hits a wayward opening tee shot.

Goal: Find a mental key that will let you forget the surrounding trouble and focus on the fairway.

Practice Procedure: Here's a drill I learned from mental coach Chuck Hogan. Each time you address the ball in practice, imagine a ring of fire a few feet in front of your ball. Now, just concentrate on hitting the ball through that big circle. Bring this image with you to the first tee and keep using it throughout the round.

When setting up, take your mind off any surrounding trouble by imagining a ring of fire to hit the ball through.

PASTA DRILL

Problem: The player experiences a great degree of tension in the arms at address.

Result: This tension causes the player to make an overly slow swing and lose a great deal of power.

Goal: To find a mental image that promotes a relaxed address position and a syrupy, yet accelerating, Sam Snead–like swing.

Practice Procedure: When setting up to hit the ball, imagine that your arms are made of spaghetti, as the late, great teacher Claude Harmon taught me to do. You want the arms to be comfortably extended and relaxed, never rigid or tight. The spaghetti image will put you on the right track.

To alleviate body tension, imagine that your arms are made of spaghetti.

RIGHT-HIP-POCKET DRILL

Problem: The player's right hip freezes on the backswing, hindering his or her ability to turn and create what I call the X-Factor, mentioned earlier.

Result: There's a dramatic loss of power in the player's swing.

Goal: To discover a swing key that will encourage the right hip to turn fluidly and allow for a free and powerful coiling action.

Practice Procedure: When hitting practice shots, follow the example set by two-time British Open champion Greg Norman. He thinks "RHP" (right hip pocket) to encourage a clockwise coiling action of the right hip on the backswing.

Think about turning your right hip pocket clockwise to help promote a stronger coil in the backswing.

BETHLEHEM STEEL DRILL

Problem: The player's left hand and wrist break down in the hitting area.

Result: The player just cannot hit a powerful shot, off the tee or from the fairway.

Goal: To discover a mental image that will allow the left wrist to stay firm through impact.

Imagine that the back of your left hand and wrist are made of steel to encourage the proper impact position.

Practice Procedure: Imagine that your left hand and wrist are made out of super-hard Bethlehem Steel. This mental image will encourage a firm left-hand position, a slightly open clubface position, and a fade shot. I learned this concept from Claude Harmon, thanks to the time he spent with Ben Hogan, but all great instructors know the importance of a solid left wrist through impact. My great friend Ken Venturi always told me the main job of the left wrist was to not break down before impact. Ken, a former U.S. Open champion, was one of the greatest ball-strikers I ever watched. I've written before that the left thumb also releases down through and past impact. That's a little add-on to the flat left wrist at impact. I have my students practice lots of small shots with different clubs until they gain the feel of this action and then master it.

JOHN DALY'S POWER-DRIVE DRILL

Problem: The player fails to accelerate the club in the impact zone. He "pecks" at the ball.

Result: The player's drives lack power and he loses distance off the tee.

Goal: To discover a mental image that will help promote a tension-free swing, a longer flat spot (which is stressed at my Jim McLean Golf School), and added clubhead speed in the impact zone.

Imagine you want to explode a cap on the back of the ball to promote high clubhead speed and a powerful hitting action.

Practice Procedure: When practicing, use this mental-image drill that John Andrisani shared with me after working on *Grip It and Rip It!*—a book he wrote with John Daly, the originator of the drill. Let me now share it with you.

Visualize a child's toy gun cap taped to the back of the golf ball. Then, each time you swing, try and hit the ball so solidly that the imaginary cap explodes. Practicing with this image in mind will allow you to swing more powerfully and propel the ball longer distances. So take it with you to the golf course.

SHAFT-TO-SHOULDER DRILL

Problem: The player concentrates so hard on the ball that, ironically, he decelerates the club through the impact zone and never completely follows through. The player might even stop just after impact.

Result: The player never reaches his full power-potential.

Goal: Discover a swing key that will promote an accelerating through-swing action.

Practice Procedure: Before you swing, imagine the clubshaft hitting your left shoulder at the finish. This actually happens when Tiger Woods, Sergio Garcia, John Daly, Davis Love III, and other power hitters finish their swing. This image will encourage you to whip the club through the ball at high speed and pick up distance in the process.

Harry "Lighthorse" Cooper used this drill when we taught together at Westchester Country Club in Rye, New York. I watched Harry use this drill often and with great success. Since then I've had many students work on the same drill. Try it and you'll be amazed at the freedom and speed it forces into your swing. Harry, a thirty-seven-time winner on the PGA Tour and a Hall of Fame member, would say: "Hit your neck, quickly." See if it doesn't work for you.

To promote acceleration, think of finishing the swing with the clubshaft on your left shoulder. This image will encourage a powerful through-impact action.

HIGH-SHOT DRILL

Problem: The player feels that he or she has no chance to hit a shot over a tree, even when there's a nice cushion of grass beneath the ball and the shot is only short-iron distance.

Result: This negative attitude has a bad effect on the player's ability to hit the ball high.

Goal: Find a mental link to promote this shot.

Practice Procedure: When practicing this shot in an area of the range that features trees, or on the course, take a page out of golf instructor John Anselmo's lesson book. Anselmo is the man who taught Tiger Woods from the age of ten until eighteen.

To help students learn to hit the ball high with the greatest of ease, Anselmo has them conjure up an image of a rocket launch at the Kennedy Space Center. This may sound like something for Star Trek fans, but the fact is it will make practice fun, particularly for juniors. Furthermore, implanting this image into your brain helps you make the correct swing actions, particularly through impact when you need to stay behind the ball.

Imagine a rocket launch when you take your address to hit a high shot, since this image will help you make the right moves.

MAGIC-CARPET DRILL

Problem: The player swings the club on an overly steep plane.

Result: The player hits short pitch shots fat. You can't apply the steep, short-follow-through action used for recovering from rough when hitting pitches off fairway grass, especially when it's wet.

Goal: To learn how to swing the club down on a more level and streamlined path, so that you avoid taking deep divots and hitting the ball short of your intended target.

Practice Procedure: Before swinging, see yourself hitting the ball cleanly off a piece of carpet, with the sole of the club brushing it through impact. Use this same mental key when hitting off fairway grass, since it will promote a shallow angle of attack, clean contact, a fluid follow-through, and a nicely lofted pitch shot.

Imagining that you're hitting the ball off a carpet will help you hit clean, lofted pitch shots.

WINDOW-OF-OPPORTUNITY DRILL

Problem: The player has trouble "threading the needle" when trying to hit a shot between the branches of trees.

Result: His trouble shots hit trees and he scores double-bogey frequently.

Goal: To discover a mental drill that will aid in the execution of this shot.

Practice Procedure: Go to a part of the range that features a few trees, or practice in a wooded area of the course in the quiet of an afternoon. Next, drop twenty balls on the ground. Then, instead of addressing the ball quickly and playing a "hit-and-hope" shot, follow the example set by one of the all-time great trouble players: Seve Ballesteros.

In practice, Seve always looked closely at the branches and searched for "windows" to hit through—obviously, the bigger the better. If you're lucky enough to discover more than one possible escape route, mentally visualize a ball flying through each one, decide which route is the least risky, then match a club and swing to the shot that played best in your mind's eye. Because Seve worked on this drill, he was more able to quickly find a window of escape when he got himself in tree-trouble on the course. So will you.

Imagining windows in
the trees will help you
hit shots like this.

RULER DRILL

Problem: The player feels lost when hitting a basic greenside bunker shot.

Result: Sometimes he or she leaves the ball in the bunker, while other times it flies over the green.

Goal: The player wants to discover a mental key that has nothing to do with technique, but will allow him or her to cut out the proper slice of sand.

Practice Procedure: Imagine a four-inch ruler stretching back from behind the ball. The one-inch mark is closest to the ball, while the four-inch mark is farther away. Additionally, imagine a ruler in front of the ball, and understand that the clubhead must pass underneath the golf ball and drive through the sand for about another four inches.

Each time you practice a bunker shot, visualize the rulers. That way, the bounce of the club will contact the sand, skid down under the ball, and then slide through the sand beneath it.

Imagining a four-inch ruler will help you hit down under the ball and through it. You can also imagine a ruler of the same length behind the ball.

BURIED-LIE DRILL

Problem: The player has trouble hitting out of buried lies. He or she tries to follow-through, or has no idea on how to play a buried-lie shot.

Result: The player fails to save par from greenside bunkers.

Goal: To find a drill that will teach you the proper impact action and allow you to make recovering a given.

Imagining that you're hitting a low rope will help you employ a hit-and-hold action through impact and recover from a buried lie.

Practice Procedure: From this type of lie, you want a square or closed clubface at address. You also want to make a compact backswing and then swing the club down sharply into the sand using a hit-and-hold action. Essentially, there is no follow-through.

Imagine that there are two stakes in the sand, with a rope or string tied loosely from one to the other. The imaginary rope should be level with your chest. Next, place a ball a couple of feet behind the imaginary stakes—on your side of the fence, so to speak. Now, set up to play a short bunker shot out of a buried lie. Swing. If you correctly used a hit-and-hold action through impact, the club should not have contacted the imaginary rope.

Gary Player still uses this drill to teach golfers how to groove the proper impact action—only he uses real stakes and real rope.

DON'T-BREAK-THE-GLASS DRILL

Problem: The player has trouble hitting the ball close to the hole out of a high-lip bunker when there's little green to work with. The reasons? His or her swing is too shallow and he or she takes too little sand.

Result: The ball is launched so low that it hits the lip or flies well past the hole.

Goal: Discover a mental-image drill that helps promote a very upright back-swing plane and a descending blow.

Practice Procedure: Pretend there's a plate-glass window behind you. This image will promote a more upright swing and allow you to take more sand, and it's the sand that lifts the ball out and over the lip.

Avoiding hitting an imaginary piece of glass behind you will promote an upright swing and help you recover from a bunker with a high lip.

BREAK-POINT DRILL

Problem: The player fails to use his imagination on long, curling putts.

Result: The player leaves these putts short of the hole and on the low side.

Goal: To find a way to read putts better, reach the hole almost every time, and occasionally sink the long "bomb."

Practice Procedure: When addressing a long putt, imagine a golf ball at the crest of the break. If you try to hit the imaginary ball, the real ball will start out on the high side of the hole and curve toward the cup.

Imagining a second ball at the crest of the break will help you hit curling putts close to the hole.

STRETCH-YOUR-IMAGINATION
DRILL *(Timeless Winner)*

Problem: The player beats balls on the range, failing to get into an on-course mind-set.

Result: When actually playing the course, he or she makes mental mistakes and lacks the imaginative power necessary to be a creative shot-maker.

Goal: To find a way to stir the imagination and become a more rounded shot-maker.

Practice Procedure: When practicing drives, fairway-wood shots, medium irons, short irons, wedges, pitches, chips, and putts, pretend that you are actually playing a shot on your home course. If you relate a practice shot to an actual course situation, you will feel more comfortable out on the course. Change your targets often.

Additionally, pretend you landed in trouble and need to bend the ball around a tree by hitting either a fade or draw recovery shot. Practice these shots, so when you're on the course you will be better able to see the same shots come to life in your mind's eye and execute them like a pro.

When practicing, imagine an actual shot that you'll need to play on the course. This pregame mental imagery enhances your practice and also readies you for the course situation, so that you will approach each "real" shot with confidence.

THREE-WORD DRILL

Problem: The player swings too fast when hitting drives.

Result: He or she loses control of the body, the club, and the shot.

Goal: To discover a verbal key and mental drill that will allow you to swing with more controlled speed.

Think of the word "smooth" to promote a solid takeaway (left), "transition" to promote a fluid weight-shift on the downswing (center), and "finish" to help you employ a balanced end-of-swing position (right).

Practice Procedure: When setting up to hit a tee shot in practice or play, do the following:

First, whisper the word *smooth* and imagine a deliberate takeaway action.

Second, whisper the word *transition* and imagine fluidly shifting weight back to your left foot on the downswing.

Third, whisper the word *finish* and imagine accelerating the club through the ball and into a balanced, end-of-swing position.

REPROGRAM DRILL

Problem: The player, although a low-handicapper, has trouble getting a bad round out of his head.

Result: His obsession has a negative effect on his next few games.

Goal: Find a mental drill that will help prevent a severe mood swing after a bad day on the links.

Practice Procedure: Take a mental "time out" for a minute or so and think of other things you need to be thankful for, such as your family. Alternatively, look around and appreciate the beauty of Mother Nature. At Doral, I might have golf visitors unwind, after they've had a bad day playing, by having them check out the iguana that hangs around our driving range. Do whatever it takes to relax, so you are ready to take a lesson or go back out on the course with a fresh and reprogrammed attitude.

Fred Couples is an example of a professional who does not let a bad round get under his skin. Fuzzy Zoeller is the same way. I wouldn't be surprised if this is because after an above-par scoring day Freddie thinks about his classic cars, namely his 1968 Shelby Mustang, and Fuzzy his Kentucky ranch. My point: You need to put things in perspective, by reminding yourself that golf's only a game.

After a bad round, try appreciating gifts from Mother Nature, like this iguana that hangs around the Jim McLean Golf School. That way, you won't take golf too seriously. Remember, it's only a game.

ACKNOWLEDGMENTS

Due to the continuing success of my first book, Golf Digest's *Book of Drills*, many people encouraged me to write a book featuring drills I have taught over the last decade. I also decided to put pen to paper, a second time, with the support and encouragement of my agent Scott Waxman, the editorial staff at Gotham Books, Bob Carney (who runs the book division at *Golf Digest* magazine), and my students, both amateur and pro.

On the amateur side, I particularly thank David McClain, whom I coached in the *Break 100* series televised by the Golf Channel, all of the juniors I have taught (including four that reached the number-one ranking), George Zahringer, and Ken Bakst, past United States Mid-Amateur champion, and movie actor students Michael Douglas and Sly Stallone.

On the pro side, I'm grateful to Tom Kite, Brad Faxon, Len Mattiace, James McLean, Cristie Kerr, Erik Compton, Peter Jacobsen, and Dana Quigley, plus many others who continue to use these drills to improve their swing. These professionals have also taught me a tremendous amount about productive practice.

Putting this comprehensive new book together, however, was not a one-man show. I owe great thanks to John Andrisani, the former senior editor of instruction at *Golf Magazine* and the author of more than thirty golf books. John is a true expert who served as my leading consultant on this project.

I also must acknowledge Yasuhiro Tanabe for helping better relay the instructional message visually through photographs. I'm grateful also to Brian Highland of Event Photography for doing some last-minute fill-in photography, and to Andrea Dudrow and Gary Perkinson for the phenomenal editing job.

In addition, I'd like to thank the many teachers and professionals that I have observed and conversed with about the ins and outs of swing technique, before and after I began instructing golfers in 1975. This long list includes Al Mengert, my first teacher; Carl Welty; Ken Venturi; Jimmy Ballard; David Leadbetter; Hank Haney; Claude Harmon Sr. and his four sons, Butch, Dick, Craig, and Billy; Jack Burke Jr.; Bob Toski; Phil Rodgers; Gardner Dickinson; Jack Grout;

Dave Collins; Harry Cooper; Tommy Bolt; Sam Snead; Ben Hogan; Gary Player; Nick Price; Lee Trevino; Jay Haas; and Jack Nicklaus.

I also thank my entire staff of fabulous teachers, most notably Chris Toulson, who is the director of instruction at my Jim McLean Golf School at the Doral Resort and Spa in Miami, and Glen Farnsworth, who has worked with me for more than twenty years. And I thank my business manager Joel Paige for his never-ending guidance.

Last, but certainly not least, I give my loving gratitude to my parents, my wife, Justine, and my two sons, Matt and Jon, for putting up with my constant research on golf.